**[WHAT'S THE FUTURE]**
OF BUSINESS?

Cover image: Mekanism
Cover design: Mekanism

This book is printed on acid-free paper. ∞

Copyright © 2013 by Brian Solis. All rights reserved.

Published by John Wiley & Sons, Inc., Hoboken, New Jersey.
Published simultaneously in Canada.

For general information about our other products and services, please contact our Customer Care Department within the United States at (800) 762-2974, outside the United States at (317) 572-3993 or fax (317) 572-4002.

Wiley publishes in a variety of print and electronic formats and by print-on-demand. Some material included with standard print versions of this book may not be included in e-books or in print-on-demand. If this book refers to media such as a CD or DVD that is not included in the version you purchased, you may download this material at http://booksupport.wiley.com. For more information about Wiley products, visit www.wiley.com.

*Library of Congress Cataloging-in-Publication Data:*

Solis, Brian.
    What's the future of business? : changing the way businesses create experiences / Brian Solis.
      p.  cm.
    ISBN 978–1–118–45653–8 (cloth); ISBN 978–1–118–45714–6 (ebk); ISBN 978–1–118–45718–4 (ebk); ISBN 978–1–118–45719–1 (ebk)
     1. Customer relations.  2. Customer services.  3. Social media.  4. Consumers.  I. Title.
    HF5415.5.S6218  2013
    658.4'06—dc23
                                         2012042066

Printed in the United States of America
10  9  8  7  6  5  4  3  2  1

# [WHAT'S THE FUTURE]
## OF BUSINESS?

CHANGING THE WAY BUSINESSES CREATE EXPERIENCES

## BRIAN SOLIS

WILEY

John Wiley & Sons, Inc.

# [ CONTENTS ]

# [ BUSINESS . . . MEET DESIGN ]

As you'll soon see, this book blends the worlds of business and design to deliver intentional experiences. You're going to notice something as you turn the pages. There's a reason the cover is what it is. The shape? That too was not by chance. *What's the Future of Business?* is a visual representation of a simple but powerful formula: business + design = intended experiences.

The book is organized by a traditional table of contents. But, you'll notice a virtual slider on the side of each chapter that visualizes a story arc to help you navigate each important theme as you go.

To help me deliver this experience required the assistance of some friends. First, the team at Mekanism, an award winning creative agency that I've had the pleasure of disrupting markets with over the years, is responsible for bringing the book to life. Next, my dear friend Hugh MacLeod (@gapingvoid) and his team at Social Object Factory transformed the thrust of each chapter into a piece of original art.

Thank you Mekanism.

Thank you Hugh and Social Object Factory.

Thank you too for picking up this book.

Let's go . . .

CHAPTER

TOTAL RECALL

# Happiness is not something you experience, it's something you remember.

—Oscar Levant

How do we ensure that our customers have an amazing customer experience? An intriguing question.

In the 1990 movie *Total Recall*, Douglas Quaid's character visits "Rekall," a company that helps people have experiences they wish they could have by implanting memories. For his vacation Quaid selects his dream experience, a trip to Mars with an added espionage package.

During his experience, Quaid is jolted awake carrying the experience back into the real world. It is later discovered that he really is the character he was hoping to become temporarily. Like Quaid, every customer desires a remarkable experience.

Why make customers cope with the ordinary?

*Total Recall* echoes the focus of this book and my day-to-day work. While implanting desirable experiences is not necessarily a metaphor for this book, creating real-world "customer experiences" is a critical role businesses must create in a new era of consumerism.

The *Total Recall* moment is waking consumers up to expect more from the businesses they support and the products they purchase. They not only expect better experiences, they believe they are entitled to them. This is an *opportunity* for your business to create positive experiences. For it is the experience that will become that measure of satisfaction and success.

# THE VOICE OF THE EMPOWERED CUSTOMER

Through technology, consumers are experiencing a validating and influential form of empowerment.

Businesses must recognize that the voice of the customer is now more powerful than ever before. Whether Facebook, Twitter, YouTube, Yelp, review sites, product forums, blogs, or Pinterest, your customers are sharing their experiences on platforms where audiences can find what others are saying about you.

## So what?

Your customers and prospects will inevitably find the negative experiences others have had. Customers will uncover the one horrendous review rather than the incredible experiences that others have had.

As customers tweet negative experiences, businesses try to respond or address the complaint. The more a company engages, and the more people gain access to social and mobile platforms, interactions accelerate and amplify. Knowing this, companies are spending more money and resources managing their online reputations. Increasingly, businesses are shifting resources until the traditional call center is replicated at social scale. Although that's inherently a good thing, the downside is that the call center becomes a notable cost center.

Perhaps this is just the new cost of doing business. In an era of connected consumerism, to earn customer attention, trust, and loyalty is a cost and an investment in relevance and relationships.

Yet even with the pervasiveness of technology, and increased customer expectations, businesses are making the same mistakes. We are not designing and implementing incredible experiences; rather, we're marketing, selling, and serving customers.

# What are customers to align with if we don't first define it? What do we want them to be a part of?

Now's the time for an investment in something more than price, performance, or value. The future of business is about creating experiences, products, programs, and processes that evoke splendor and rekindle meaningful and sincere interaction and growth.

At the center of this evolution—or (r)evolution—is *the* experience. And, the experience is everything now.

# [ ARE YOU EXPERIENCED? ]

Yes, it's time to invest in proactive experiences. If we do not, we will be forever tethered to the unproductive dance that is reacting, responding to, and solving negative experiences in real time, over time.

What if I told you that the cost of reacting to experiences is far greater than the cost of proactively defining experiences from the onset? Indeed, companies are investing in reactive engagement. And, for the most part, they can succeed in shifting negative experiences toward positive territory. However, any favorable outcome is weighed against the cost of the initial negative experience—or more importantly, the cost of how that negative experience was shared and how it ultimately impacted others. What's most startling is that businesses do not measure these numbers today. But that's about to change.

Businesses must invest in defining not only a positive experience, but also a wonderfully shareable experience. Doing so influences others to join the fray while offsetting negative inquiries and the damaging viral effects of shared negative experiences.

This is the time to reframe those negative experiences. Pushing a change from responding to negative experiences to proactively creating positive ones is everything. Why? The cost of reacting to negative experiences is completely eclipsed by the upside of creating and nurturing positive experiences at the inception.

To better understand the importance of experience requires that you first acknowledge that you are the very consumer you're trying to reach. You're not looking for just any experience, you're looking for *the* experience. Businesses that recognize and adapt to you and people like you will quickly learn how to entice you through shared values and meaningful affinity hooks . . . while never stopping to compete for relevance.

Experience is everything. And, businesses must create experiences that mean something. If necessity is the mother of invention, then vision is the father of innovation.

## #InnovateorDie

CHAPTER

1

# SORRY, WE'RE CLOSED

*How to Survive Digital Darwinism*

People never learn anything by being told, they have to find out for themselves.

—Paulo Coelho, Veronika Decides to Die

The customer journey is still evolving. How businesses react and ultimately lead the enhancement of relationships is not solely determined by technology.[1] To truly get closer to customers takes a culture of customer-centricity, empowerment, and innovation.

Saying that we need to get closer to the customer is hardly enough to convince business leaders that the customer revolution they hear about is literally steps away from their office door. I know I'm not saying anything here you don't already know. The difference is, however, that what started as a groundswell for business transformation from the bottom up has hit a ceiling. To break through it requires that someone (*read: you*) has to make the case to bring change from the top down.

Most executives don't use social networks or smart phones. Many don't even read their own email. Many won't ever read this book. So, trying to convince decision makers that this is a war fought on the battleground of technology is in and of itself fighting a losing battle.

The future of business isn't tied to the permeation of Facebook, Twitter, iPhones, and Droids, pins on Pinterest, tablets, or real-time geolocation check-ins. The future of business comes down to relevance and the ability to understand how technology affects decision making and behavior to the point where the recognition of new opportunities and the ability to strategically adapt to them becomes a competitive advantage.

But make no mistake: This is as much a technology revolution as it is a series of real-world revolutions that will eventually seize organizations, governments, and businesses.

## Change boils down to three things:

1. Listening

2. Learning

3. Adapting

# [ DISRUPTIVE TECHNOLOGY IS A CATALYST FOR CHANGE, NOT *THE* REASON ]

Look, I get it. Change is all anyone talks about today and we all know that talk is cheap. We also know that change is inevitable and that it is rarely easy. Among the greatest difficulties associated with change is the ability to recognize that change is needed at a time when we can actually do something about it. All too often, by the time we realize that change is needed and that we must shift to a new way of thinking, it is already too late. Or worse, competitors recognize the need for change before us, and we are by default pushed into a position where our next steps are impulsive or reactive rather than strategic.

The volume of emerging technology is both awe-inspiring and overwhelming. As new technology makes its way into everyday life and work flow, devices, applications, and networks, it disrupts the norm and begins to impact behavior. It is this disruptive technology that over time influences how people work, communicate, share, and make decisions.

## The question is at what point does emerging technology or new behavior become disruptive?

And, more importantly, what systems, processes, and protocols are in place that recognize disruption, assess opportunity, and facilitate the testing of new ideas?

The time to answer these questions is now.

In my last book, *The End of Business as Usual*,[2] I introduced the notion of Digital Darwinism, the evolution of consumer behavior when society and technology evolve faster than our ability to adapt. And the reality is that because of the role technology now plays in our lives, we forever compete for survival to effectively fight off Digital Darwinism.

Humility is a gift and it's needed in business now more than ever. Disruption not only faces every business, its effects are already spreading through customer markets and the channels that influence decisions and behavior.

A recent advertisement produced by Babson College cited a rather humbling statistic:

> **Over 40 percent of the companies that were at the top of the Fortune 500 in 2000 were no longer there in 2010.**

As we're often painfully reminded, history has a way of repeating itself. *Forbes* published an article in early 2011 that served as a harbinger for the turbulent and transformative times that lie ahead.[3] The opening line read,

> **The End is Near: Why 70% of the Fortune 1000 Will Be Replaced in a Few Years.**

The author cited a study published in the book *Built to Change* by Edward E. Lawler and Christopher G. Worley. The study found that between 1973 and 1983, 35 percent of the top companies in the Fortune 1000 companies were new to the list. Over the next decade from 1983 to 1993, churn jumped to 45 percent, and then soared again to an astounding 60 percent between 1993 and 2003. If the current trend continues, more than 70 percent of Fortune 1000 companies will turn over from 2003 to 2013. As the author observes, "In other words, over three-fourths of the existing captains of industry will fall from their throne."

## They include:

| | | |
|---|---|---|
| Blockbuster | Hostess | Mervyns |
| Borders | KB Toys | Pontiac |
| Compaq | Kodak | Tower Records |
| CompUSA | LIFE | Woolworths |
| E.F. Hutton | Merry-Go-Round | |

This is about the survival of both the fittest and the fitting. It takes more than a presence in new channels to improve customer experiences and relationships. It takes courage. It takes persistence to break through resistance. But, in the end, it's how you work with your leaders, or how you lead, to move toward an empowered and customer-centric culture that sets in motion real transformation.

You have a special path you must follow to set in motion the change that opens the door to improve experiences inside and outside the organization.

CHAPTER

# THE JOURNEY OF BUSINESS TRANSFORMATION

A mind that is stretched by a new experience can never go back to its old dimensions.

—Oliver Wendell Holmes, Jr.

# THERE'S A HERO IN EVERY ONE OF US

American mythologist, writer, and lecturer Joseph Campbell is lauded for his work in comparative mythology and comparative religion. In 1949, he published *The Hero with a Thousand Faces*[1] where he traced the journey (rise, death, and rebirth) of the archetypal hero. His theory suggested that all historical myths from around the world, many surviving thousands of years, share a common story, stages, and outcomes.

Over the years, Campbell's work has become known as the Hero's Journey. The journey that lies ahead for you is in many ways similar to that of Campbell's heroes:

> ❝ A hero ventures forth from the world of common day into a region of supernatural wonder: fabulous forces are there encountered and a decisive victory is won: the hero comes back from this mysterious adventure with the power to bestow boons on his fellow man. ❞

Campbell's Hero's Journey and its various interpretations have inspired everything from books and movies to video games . . . most notably the original *Star Wars* trilogy and the *Matrix* series. We can adapt this Hero's Journey to the world of change and change management and the role you play in creating a culture of transformation and innovation in your business.

As someone who recognizes the need for change, you are about to embark on an epic journey. You will encounter challenges, but with hard work, perseverance, and the support of those around you, you can also experience the same decisive victory as Campbell's heroes.

The journey is laid out in multiple stages, with the first being that of discovery followed by intelligence, communication, and formulation. This book covers discovery and lays out a chart for your next steps.

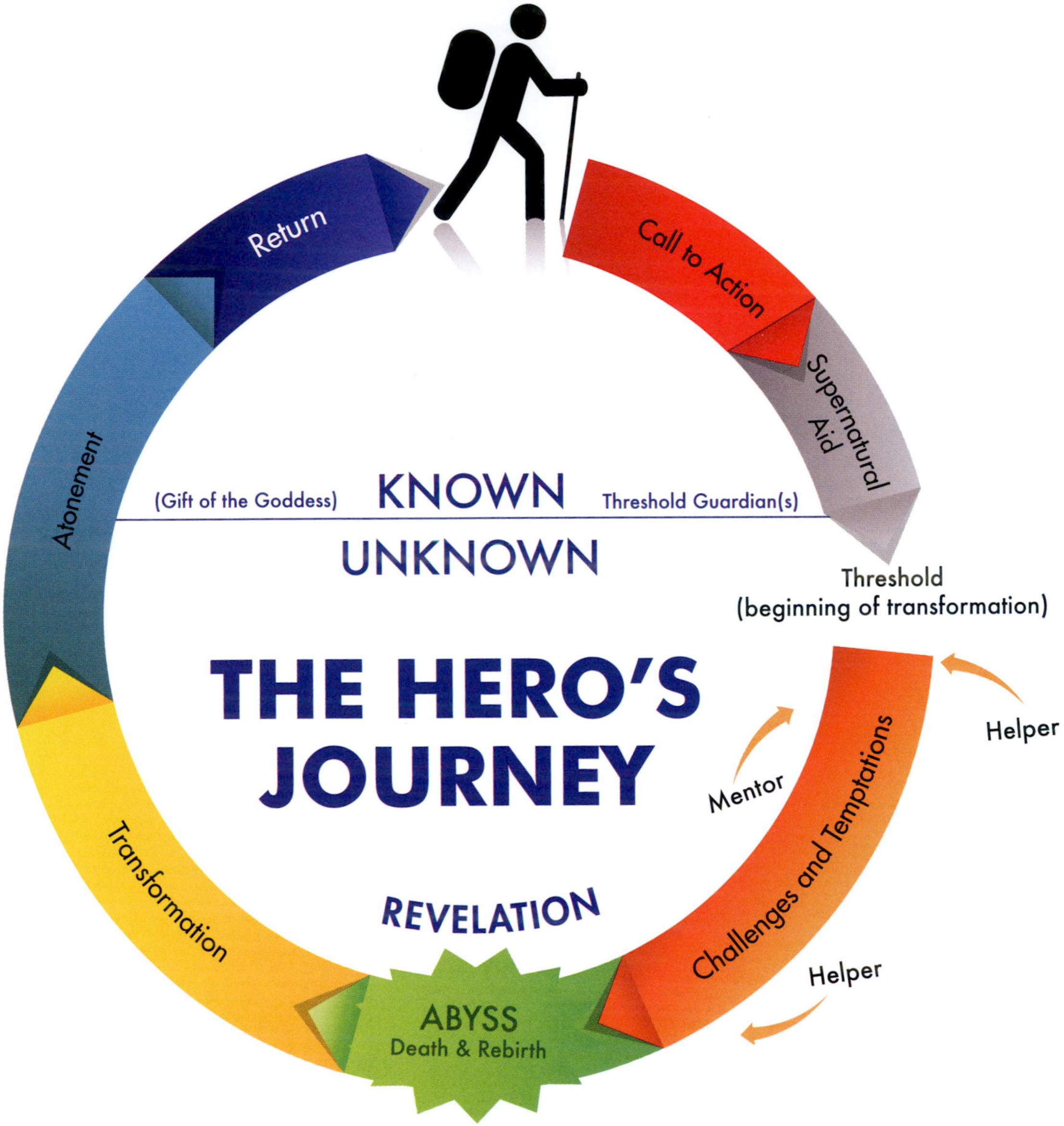

THE HERO'S JOURNEY

KNOWN

UNKNOWN

(Gift of the Goddess) — Threshold Guardian(s)

Return

Call to Action

Supernatural Aid

Threshold
(beginning of transformation)

Atonement

Helper

Mentor

Challenges and Temptations

Helper

Transformation

REVELATION

ABYSS
Death & Rebirth

The reward is business growth achieved through an enriched customer experience. The path to get there is not easy, but this is why it's called the Hero's Journey. Not everyone can lead the way.

Too often, the customer's experience of a brand is an afterthought among many businesses. To bring the experience front and center will take nothing short of internal transformation. But, every journey to transformation must begin somewhere. Acknowledging that the world is changing is certainly a start. But how customers' behavior is changing, how it's impacting decision making, and how that decision making is affecting the business landscape is what must be documented, communicated, and shared within the organization. How your customer behavior is evolving is already impacting your bottom line and it's becoming more profound every day.

# THE GREAT MYTH OF TECHNOLOGY

While everyone thinks they already know that technology is changing behavior, the reality is that assumptions and blind faith are still playing a role in how businesses are approaching these changes. Many experts believe that mobile and social networks are the new channels for engagement. They place their bets on the number of users each network boasts, as well as by the amount of attention press and bloggers pay to what's hot.

However, experts cannot tell you the role certain networks play in the customer's decision-making cycle, aka the customer journey. Nor can they pinpoint the economic impact of activity or conversations on the business before, during, and after the transaction. That is why the answer to the question of what the return on investment (ROI) of these initiatives is, is elusive to them. Instead they come up with new terminology to support their blind faith.

Technology is not *the* answer, it's part of the answer. Many social media enthusiasts are convincing businesses, governments, and nonprofits to use social media based on this blind faith supported by soft metrics that for all intents and purposes is old marketing guised as newfound engagement. Just because a business is embracing new technology doesn't mean that it is creating meaningful, productive, or measurable experiences.

In many cases, my research shows that expansion into new networks is actually causing social blindness (the new media equivalent to banner or advertising blindness). It also causes brand dilution because the experience is the furthest thing from defined, reinforced, or integrated. This happens because organizations are siloed. No surprise here. And, by nature, these silos contribute to the problem of disconnected or competing experiences. Businesses are often experimenting with new technologies independent of the overall business efforts. Meaning, what one side of the company is saying and doing is different from the other. Therefore, the experience starts to work against the brand, or the brand promise.

It's not enough to *know* consumers are changing how they communicate, connect, discover, and, in turn, purchase. It's not enough to adopt the technologies and networks they're using. It's not enough to even fight for attention for these new networks. Your path begins with discovery and rethinking the new customer journey.

# This is the end of business as usual.

But to get anywhere, you have to prove it.

If you can collect and interpret the data and behaviors of your customers, they will lead to insights and the confidence necessary to convince the skeptics and the fearful. The truth is that the market votes with its dollars and those dollars are already being siphoned away from the inputs you have in place today.

By entering the journey with the intention of discovery, you will learn where you're losing dollars and the new places and supporting strategies where they can be earned and re-earned. Dollars are being increasingly earned and spent in new touch points. Discovery unlocks information. And information is empowering. Your work will demonstrate which side of the dollar you're on now and how to be on the right side of revenue and relationships over the next several years.

The journey before you is great. The remainder of this book walks you through the dynamics of discovery to guide you to seek answers. But before we continue on this path, you must have a view of the overall picture. Let's walk in the journey of our customers to define their journey. Doing so will give us perspective on where we need to focus when you've finished reading.

CHAPTER

3

[ **MEET THE NEW GENERATION OF CUSTOMERS . . . GENERATION C** ]

We live in a time where brands are people and people are brands.

With every day that passes, Generation Y, also known as the *Millennials*, become far more important to the economy than we can realize. Generation Y is considered to be those individuals born in the early 1980s to 2000s. They're important because a gap exists between how Gen Y communicates and connects and how businesses, educators, and governments approach them, and it's widening. In this era of Digital Darwinism, a time when society and technology are evolving faster than many organizations can adapt, we must realize that customer landscapes are not only changing, they're evolving beyond our grasp today.

Do leaders realize that although they act like they're talking to customers they already know, they are in fact talking to strangers?

Without understanding what matters to customers and why, without learning their behavior or decision-making cycles, and without empathy, we cannot create a meaningful and engaging customer experience. And, because this emerging class of connected consumers is so critical to the future of economics, this is a time when decision makers should stop looking at people through a lens of demographics and instead start designing experiences and outcomes based on interests and behavior. We cannot create experiences based on where they are to us nor can we expect them to use them.

# So, how well do you know Gen Y? Let's find out . . .

**Here are some interesting data points that will help turn these would-be strangers into potential partners and customers:[1]**

- Gen Y will form 75 percent of the work force by 2025 and are actively shaping corporate culture and expectations.[2] Only 11 percent define having a lot of money as a definition of success.

- Only 7 percent of Gen Y works for a Fortune 500 company as start-ups dominate the work force for this demographic. Gen Y'ers expect larger organizations to hear their voice and recognize their contributions . . . increasing the need for an "intrapreneurial" culture.

- Millennials watch TV with two or more electronic devices.[3]

- Millennials trust strangers over friends and family. They lean on user-generated experiences (UGE) for purchase decisions.

- They are three times as likely to follow a brand over a family member in social networks.

- Sixty-six percent will look up a store if they see a friend check in.

- Seventy-three percent have earned and used virtual currency.

- Gen Y'ers believe that other consumers care more about their opinions than companies do—that's why they share their opinions online.

- Gen Y'ers are more connected on Facebook than average users, managing a social graph of 696 Facebook friends versus the 140 maintained by everyday people.

- Twenty-nine percent find love through Facebook while 33 percent are dumped via TXT or Wall posts (SRS)—abbreviation for seriously.

# WIDENING THE VIEW FROM GENERATION Y TO GENERATION C

We often think about social media or mobile devices as the conduits to successful customer engagement. After all, that's where attention is focused.

It takes more than technology to reach Generation Y. It takes understanding and empathy. That's why these times are so significant: A growing number of your customers influence and are influenced in ways unfamiliar to us. How they communicate and connect, how they learn, discover, and share, how they make decisions, and how they take action are different from the generations before them.

So why wouldn't a presence on any one of the most important social networks or mobile platforms clinch our future relevance in business?

The answer lies in how we view their worth in the customer ecosystem. We assume to extremes: These networks will either make us or they are completely irrelevant. The problem, though, is in our perspective. You are a small business owner. You are an executive or a manager within a small-to-medium sized business. You are an executive with a global enterprise. You are an entrepreneur. You have a responsibility to not only your business, but your employees, vendors, and also your customers equally. To see them through one lens is, well, too clouded. But to see people for who they are and what defines them, that's where the future of business and relevance begins.

How is this different from the consumers whom you've known over the years? For starters, they're connected. Yes, they're on Facebook and Twitter. But, it's more than that. Smart phones, tablets, ultraportable laptops, and whatever's next . . . technology is becoming an extension of humanity. But it's not the case for everyone and that's part of the challenge. Having multiple consumer behaviors to cater to forces organizations to think differently about this group of connected consumers than the traditional consumers they've gotten to know over the years. However, we have to look beyond Millennials or the younger Generation Z that follows them.

I refer to this new group of connected consumers as *Generation C*.[4] It covers Gen Y, Generation Z, as well as anyone else among Generation X, Boomers, and Matures who's crossed over to the digital lifestyle. This new consumer category that our businesses must serve is something altogether bigger than any demographic. This is the dawn of Generation C,[5] where "C" represents a connected society based on interests and behavior. Gen C is not an age group—it is a way of life.

Gen C'ers are not bound by age; they're not defined by income, ethnicity, or education, either. These consumers do not surf the web like other customers. They live and breathe in social networks and use mobile devices as their windows to the world. They don't learn or make decisions like their traditional counterparts. Gen C lives the digital lifestyle and unites demographics around interests and behavior.

Gen C'ers are different from any segment you've addressed in the past. What you think they want and what they truly value are worlds apart. Whether we get it or not, they're always on and to reach them takes an altogether different approach. And, when you compare the size of the market for traditional consumers versus Generation C over the next few years, one of the two segments is growing while the other is shrinking.

If markets are shifting, think about how strategies are affected for a moment. Over time, but increasingly on a daily basis, greater emphasis will be placed on connected consumerism and the technology and channels they embrace over traditional marketing programs. As a result, new skill sets will be, and already are, required to engage Gen C. As a result, budgets are moving from traditional to new digital initiatives. So, which side of the dollar or investment do you want to be on? The side where budgets are dwindling or the side where demand and resulting budgets are growing?

# DIFFERENT TIMES CALL FOR DIFFERENT MEASURES

For some, Gen C is a small but not insignificant share over your current opportunity. For others, Gen C'ers are a dominant source of influence and revenue. What's consistent is that they're growing as a market segment. And, they rely on the shared experiences of like-minded strangers to guide their actions.

To Gen C, experience is everything. What they feel about your products and services now and over time is shared through these connected networks. They know that other Gen C'ers rely on their shared experiences to find resolution. If you're not proactively designing the experience they have or defining the journey that they will embark on, you cannot influence the experience that's shared about your brand.

**As you align your business objectives and strategies over the next year, start with the experience that you want your connected customer, and all customers for that matter, to embrace.**

**1** Walk in their shoes.

**2** Learn how they connect and communicate.

**3** Discover how they discover.

**4** Uncover their preferences and expectations, and more importantly, what they value.

**5** Design marketing, service, engagement, and product strategies that add value.

**6** Lead the journey today and tomorrow.

The chance that Gen C will find you through traditional channels grows fainter every day. But that's not as ominous as it sounds. Opportunity is abundant.

The only thing that separates you from connected customers is your view of them, their awareness, and the channels that they rely on for engagement and fulfillment. The rest is opportunity and the relentless pursuit of engaging, creating remarkable experiences, and delivering value. Now is the time to recognize how your customer landscape is shifting and to what extent traditional and connected consumers discover and make decisions differently.

CHAPTER

# THE NEW CUSTOMER HIERARCHY

In real life, the most practical advice for leaders is not to treat pawns like pawns, nor princes like princes, but all persons like persons.

—James MacGregor Burns

Have you attended a concert where it seemed that everyone in the audience was holding up a phone to snap pictures or shoot videos? Or perhaps you noticed people looking down at their mobile devices, rather than focusing on the show. What's the point, right? After all, going to an event is about being in the moment. It's about enjoying the experience to the fullest.

Those individuals may seem distracted, but they are very much a part of the occasion. Multitasking is a way of life for them. But this isn't just a love affair with smart phones and tablets. These "always on" audiences are sharing real-world experiences as they happen with their friends on Facebook, Twitter, Instagram, and Socialcam. And their friends respond in real time, participating in the experience.

These Gen C'ers are defining a new landscape for engagement. They're becoming increasingly networked with everyday individuals amassing hundreds or even thousands of friends and followers in every network. What they say matters more than ever before as word of mouth evolves from one-to-one to one-to-many conversations. Shared experiences are a formidable currency in this network economy where an audience with an audience of its own continues to grow in influence. And, it's this influence that is changing how consumers and organizations connect.

We are witnessing a "C" change (C for customer) in the balance of power between consumers and businesses: it's transforming the face of engagement and redefining the parameters of how businesses market and serve their consumers.

# A NEW ERA OF SOCIAL SERVICE: PROMOTING THE EXPERIENCES OF CUSTOMERS

Have you ever noticed that it's mainly social media experts who address their problems with companies on Twitter? Why? It's because they figured out that by leaning on the reach and volume of their networks, they can get attention and make a difference. They also jump ahead of traditional service queues by making the infraction public. Businesses that respond do so to first limit the extent of negative sentiment, and some engage to truly change and improve perception.[1]

You've probably seen, or contributed to, tweets, blog posts, Facebook updates, or YouTube videos that share negative experiences about people, products, or companies. While some question the value of engaging customers in social networks, the simple truth is that social media didn't unlock the ability to share experiences. Word of mouth has always been around, whether good or bad. Customers have taken to social networks so they can have a say in how other consumers view an organization. Additionally, customers are learning to take to these channels to voice their frustrations or to force companies to listen, respond to, and resolve problems directly.

At the center of this evolving customer landscape are shared experiences. People share everything. And whether we believe it or not, the activity around these shared experiences influences the impressions and behaviors of other consumers in social networks. To what effect can be debated.[2]

Sites like Klout, Kred, and PeerIndex now measure social media activity and translate it into an "influence score." Unless users specifically opt out, they are already indexed and ranked by these scores, which for better or for worse introduce a social consumer hierarchy. These measures of digital influence are quite literally becoming a new standard for consumer marketing and service. And connected consumers know it.

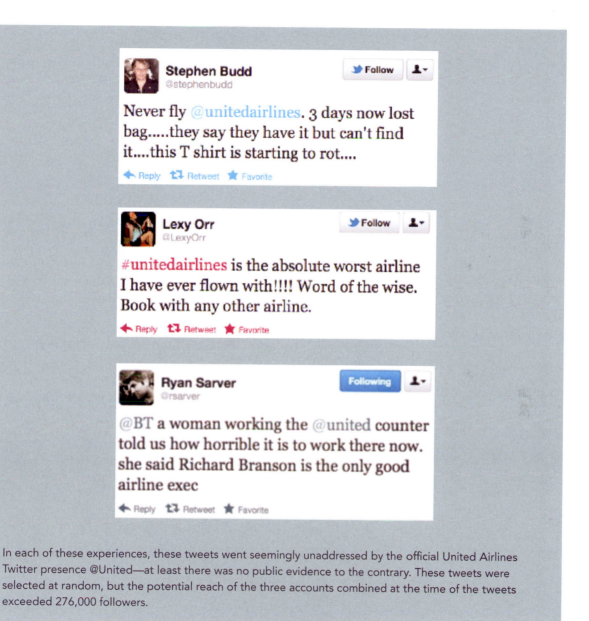

Never fly @unitedairlines. 3 days now lost bag.....they say they have it but can't find it....this T shirt is starting to rot....

#unitedairlines is the absolute worst airline I have ever flown with!!!! Word of the wise. Book with any other airline.

@BT a woman working the @united counter told us how horrible it is to work there now. she said Richard Branson is the only good airline exec

In each of these experiences, these tweets went seemingly unaddressed by the official United Airlines Twitter presence @United—at least there was no public evidence to the contrary. These tweets were selected at random, but the potential reach of the three accounts combined at the time of the tweets exceeded 276,000 followers.

United Airlines missed an opportunity to connect with Ryan Sarver, who alone had over 275,000 followers at the time. The person he was corresponding with, @BT, who also tweeted a negative experience with United, had more than 420,000 followers at the time. In the social consumer hierarchy, these two very connected customers are certainly worthy of engagement. Combined, these two individuals eclipsed @United's followers on Twitter by almost six times.

Alternatively, other airlines like Virgin America, JetBlue, and Southwest, as well as other businesses spanning almost every industry, use social networks as a way to engage dissatisfied customers. Doing so acknowledges that the voice of the customer is important and also often converts negative situations into positive outcomes. Customers often follow up complaints with praise.

Many businesses also take a very important next step, which is to acknowledge happy customers. This form of positive reinforcement serves as a form of "unmarketing" where consumers feel appreciated and are encouraged to share all that they love about the business, product, and overall experience.

Individuals with the largest, most loyal, or actively engaged networks form a powerful consumer landscape. What they share contributes to a collective brand or service experience that without engagement is left for the connected audiences to define.

The connected consumer can become a formidable foe or ally for any organization. As such, the proactive investment in positive experiences now represents a modern and potentially influential form of consumer marketing and service. But to engage in the new realm of digital influence will take more than tweets or participating in social media conversations. Connected audiences demand that marketers and executives alike rethink the entire customer experience pre-, during, and posttransaction.

# THE BROKEN LINK OF SOCIAL MEDIA CUSTOMER SERVICE

For all that disruptive technology is doing to change business for the better, it's not yet enough. Ask executives what their priority business goals are for the next year and I'm sure you'll see some element of customer-focus. The challenge that exists for any organization trying to get closer to customers lies in its customer-centricity.[3] Sure, products and services count for almost everything. And yes, we're learning about the importance of being proactive. But if a customer has a question, wishes to provide feedback, or needs help, this often results in buyers' remorse or resentment.

In an effort to improve customer service and manage costs, companies began investing in automated solutions to improve the efficiency of customer engagement: sophisticated voice recognition systems to alleviate the hardship of pushing buttons to direct calls; improved call transferring that lessens the frequency of getting dropped; web forms, click-to-talk applets, and email ensure that the first round of automated replies you receive look more human than ever before. And, internal metrics are designed to incentivize representatives to reduce the amount of time it takes to get issues resolved. This eliminates the need to build comfort, confidence, and trust in each call. No, I'm not serious about this improving service. But this is the reality that a majority of human beings experience to pursue satisfaction or resolution.

Whereas the last mile of service is where a representative delivers a service to customers, the first mile is where experiences begin. The first mile of customer engagement is the postcommerce or posttransaction strategy that creates an ongoing experience to keep customers happy now and over time. Doing so sparks positive word of mouth and in turn influences decisions in the dynamic customer journey that defines the new era of connected consumerism.

# But, if getting closer to customers is a key objective, why do many businesses neglect the first mile of customer experiences?

When you look at how social media is utilized inside most organizations, you find that there's a broken link between social media marketing and customer service. In fact, the majority of time, money, and resources are invested in marketing—not in supporting customers through engagement on social networks.

If a customer shares an experience or asks a question online, the ability for marketing to address it is certainly there. The trouble is that most of the time, the person or team managing social networks cannot effectively provide resolution or satisfaction. And there isn't an internal process or technology platform that connects customers using social networks to customer service. This leads to a phenomenon that I call the *Broken Link of Customer Engagement* or the *Social Arc Effect*.[4]

If consumers have the power to act as either an extended sales force or as detractors, a change in priority is necessary.

Just because a company does not have a dedicated customer service person on social networks doesn't mean that customers understand the difference. To consumers, a Facebook page or a Twitter handle *is* the brand. Customers do not see silos; they see one company. It's up to the social media team to connect the dots instead of people tasked with managing social aspects of the business in a silo existing on its own.

Customer-centricity starts with recognizing that customer experiences are owned by the customer. As much as businesses attempt to integrate great experiences into product features and design, the ultimate experience unfolds at the point of engagement. In social media, because most activity is run out of the marketing department, when customers express discontent, praise, or simply require direction in the social networks of any brand, their outreach is initially received by the community manager or the representative agency/consultant.

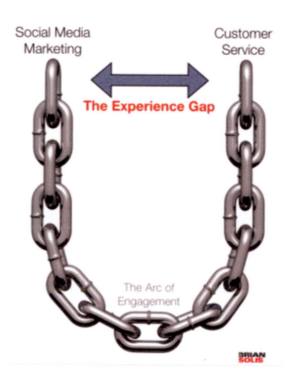

Social Media Marketing

Customer Service

**The Experience Gap**

The Arc of Engagement

BRIAN SOLIS

Depending on internal processes or the rules of engagement, chances are that customer sentiment and real-time needs will be overlooked, and as such, become the victim of a siloed enterprise.[5] In reality, marketing doesn't talk to customer service, or any other function for that matter, and customer service, without design, isn't aggressive in staffing up dedicated engagement across the social web.

A study conducted by Satmetrix in mid-2012 revealed that less than half of the companies it surveyed tracked and followed up on customer feedback in social media. An astonishing 28 percent do not track or respond, leaving customers to question their value to the businesses that they support. That lack of acknowledgment or engagement leaves the door wide open to competitive courtship.

# CONNECTING THE DOTS IN SOCIAL MEDIA TO IMPROVE EXPERIENCES

Acquisition of customers through social networks is only part of the story. The brilliance of social networks is the opportunity to transform negative experiences into positive outcomes. Conversations inspire opportunities for product refinement or innovation to create remarkable experiences from the onset.

In 2007, I wrote a piece on how social media presented an opportunity to turn customer service into the "new" marketing, because retention is the new acquisition. For companies experimenting with social media, it's time to break it out of the traditional call center and create a proactive group of expert agents. While social media is yet another channel for agents to engage customers such as chat, email, and phones, the reality is that it requires a different philosophy to effectively manage relationships and agent performance.

Time to resolution, cost per engagement, NPS, wait time . . . these are metrics of an aging era. Advocacy, referrals, positive endorsements, reviews, loyalty, these are the metrics that can be directly linked to social customer service among many other tangible outcomes, including return on investment (ROI).

The first mile of customer satisfaction, keeping you and me happy, must begin with reflection and introspection. To become customer-centric requires a change in how we value customers and the role they play in the decision-making cycles of those who make choices based on the shared experiences of others. The first mile is then paved through listening, governance, and engagement.

The Arc Effect is a visual representation of what is and what could be. Completing the arc should be a priority for businesses striving to be more customer-centric. To truly improve relationships and unlock advocacy requires that social media strategists work with customer

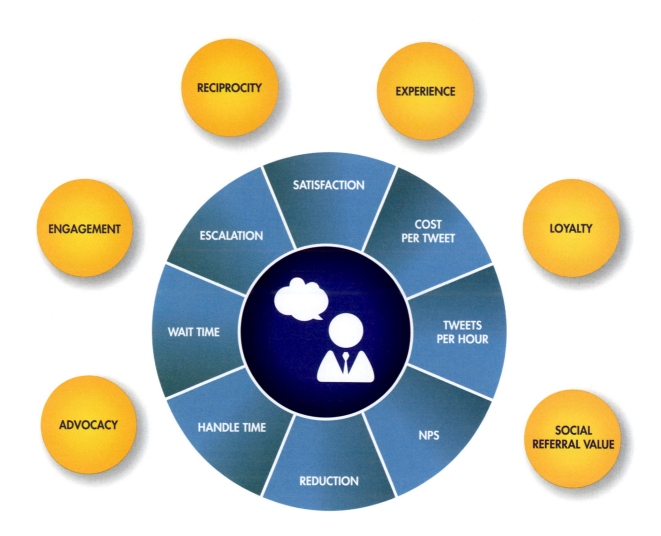

Even though companies are engaging in social networks, they do not want to talk to you and it shows in their metrics.

strategists to create an integrated series of processes and defined roles and responsibilities. Doing so delivers a holistic experience that turns customers into stakeholders and stakeholders into protagonists of aspirational experiences. This is where your efforts should begin.

# Answer this question: What is the experience you want customers to have?

In the end, no amount of responses can fix a broken product or service. Businesses must now proactively invest in the experiences they want customers to have and use new technology to measure the alignment of intended experiences versus shared experiences.

In the future, the new customer hierarchy will either work for you or against you. And if customers are going to talk about you, then give them something to talk about. Experiences are now the new "relationship."

CHAPTER

5

# THE DIM LIGHT AT THE END
# OF THE FUNNEL

The only source of knowledge is experience.

—Albert Einstein

Over the years, businesses have developed sales, marketing, and service strategies around the sales funnel.[1] The model of awareness, interest, desire, and action describes the likely steps a customer may take in making a decision. If only the world were that simple.

It was assumed that the linear path of the funnel would continue despite the evolution of technology and behavior. But regardless, a journey as it migrates from consideration to evaluation to purchase to a state of loyalty and ultimately advocacy isn't that simple to earn, unfortunately (or fortunately). The process of customer engagement requires dedicated monitoring, not just listening, to shepherd people along this delicate path. For at any moment, consumer attention, interest, and the resulting action could go astray without proper supervision or leadership.

This is why investing in creating the desired experience before, during, and after it's experienced is so critical to the future of relationships and word of mouth. If people can't connect with your intentions, then they can't contribute to intended outcomes.

# FUNNEL VISION: WITHOUT AWARENESS THERE CAN BE NO CONSIDERATION

The customer journey goes beyond a simple sales funnel. Yet it is the funnel model that dictates how businesses invest in product development, sales, marketing, and service strategies.

Businesses today invest to varying degrees and effectiveness in marketing, advertising, and communications programs. However, customer attention isn't a switch that toggles on and off—it is a state of perpetual engagement. The blaring noise that customers continually experience has forced them to adapt. Second nature acts as a defense mechanism to tune out the constant barrage of marketing messages and clever campaigns. Awareness at the top of the funnel is elusive but the stakes have never been higher.

But what if businesses were investing their time and resources in the wrong places? What if where we think we can get customers to notice us is not at all where their attention is actually focused?

These questions will reveal a new journey to embark on. The truth is that what we know and what we need to know are separated by an unfolding reality that requires immediate intervention.

In a narrow, but honest, view businesses are designed to pull customers into the funnel. Strategists see people as targets and use marketing, not products or exceptional experiences, as bait. It's assumed that customers make decisions that follow a series of linear and equally weighted steps to find and purchase your products and then later advocate to anyone and everyone on your behalf.

# THE CLUSTER FUNNEL

**In reality, the funnel is less about AIDA (awareness, interest, decision, and action—we'll also add loyalty to give businesses the benefit of the doubt). Instead it is a superficially designed production with six distinct acts:**

**1**  **The Persuasion:** Convince the prospects that they need your product without considering their need, experience, or the reward. This is done through clever marketing and advertising. Contests and campaigns also raise awareness to create need or the perception of it.

**2**  **The Hook:** Emphasize the reasons to buy in the moment rather than the long-term relationship or outcome. Packaging, price, rebate, gifts, and promotions are often the lure necessary to convert browsing into action.

**3**  **The Exchange:** Convert the prospect into a customer. This is the moment someone officially becomes a stakeholder. There is an exchange beyond the payment for a product. Value must now be delivered on both sides of the relationship.

**4**  **The Distance:** The distance here is that the space between the brand promise and the customer experience begins to spread. If a customer encounters anything negative, the distance is then measured by the steps it takes for a customer and business to connect and bring about resolution.

**5**  **The Reenchantment:** Realizing that the customer experience is not completely understood, this stage is dedicated to finding ways to keep customers interested and coming back. Strategies include discounts, promotions, exclusive offers, loyalty programs, and beta tests, among others.

**6** **The Governance:** Once customers are enticed or in some cases ensnared, the relationship moves into a state of customer relationship management. You're now forever known as a number with a record on file. Conversations are now managed as tickets and placed within a queue for engagement and resolution. Your service level and attention level can be tied to your position within the customer hierarchy.

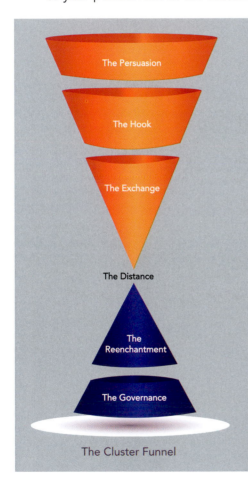

The Persuasion

The Hook

The Exchange

The Distance

The Reenchantment

The Governance

The Cluster Funnel

Revisiting Total Recall for a moment, the awakening customer has already altered the steps emphasized in the funnel. Technology introduces a sense of liberty that reminds each and every one of us that as strategists and decision makers, we have much to learn.

Your market has already been disrupted. Through an unforgiving series of technology revolutions in an era of individual empowerment, your customers are not only more informed, their expectations have grown. The "C" change in consumerism has ushered in a genre of connected consumers. As a result, your customers are learning about you and your competitors differently. How they make decisions does not follow a linear path. How they are influenced and in turn influence others is profound in its reach and effect.

What was once a simplistic representation of a fluted customer journey is in fact much more dynamic and connected. Learning how to uncover the moment of truth and shape experiences will set the stage for more meaningful outcomes and relationships.

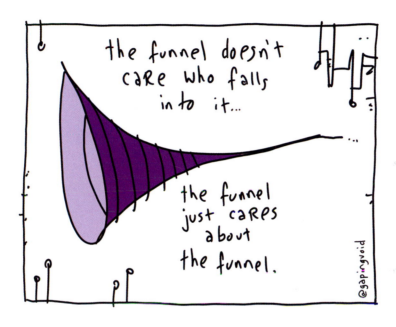

Experience is not what happens to you. It is what you do with what happens to you.

—Aldous Huxley

When we talk about real time, we often think about rapid engagement and response. Doing so misses the splendor of what real time truly offers: the ability to listen, learn, and adapt. In many ways, though, we need to move faster than real time in order to get in front of it. Otherwise we're forever locked into a rhythm of reacting rather than leading.

Welcome to the moment of truth . . . a series of four stages where customers take actions that move them toward or away from you.

You are competing in real time and at the right time. This "right" time is often referred to as the *moment of truth*. The MOT is that crucial moment when your customer decides at some point along the journey to select you or stay with you. In a real-time world, the "urgency of now" is that moment of truth that happens, well, right now.

On August 28, 1963, at the Lincoln Memorial, Washington, DC, Dr. Martin Luther King Jr. shared with us his dream, a dream that united people, hope, aspiration, and ambition to convey the urgency of now.[1]

> " We have also come to this hallowed spot to remind America of the fierce urgency of Now. This is no time to engage in the luxury of cooling off or to take the tranquilizing drug of gradualism. Now is the time to make real the promises of democracy. "

That's what the urgency of now is all about, at least in business, anyway.

# In the moment of truth, how do you fare and what shared experiences are awaiting your customer?

If it's not defined, then the urgency of now and the moment of truth will be your undoing. The thing about technology is that it connects us. It binds us together through actions, words, and shared experiences. The moments of truth are therefore paramount pre- and postpurchase. As people research, read reviews, tweets, and blog posts, ask and answer questions, watch videos, and simply learn from the experiences of others, these moments of truth require study and definition.

As you begin to research the journey ahead, you realize the number of opportunities there are for continued engagement before, during, and after transactions. Without continuous engagement, decisions are either made for or against you in the moment. Understanding how to add value directly and indirectly shifts decisions in your favor. On top of that, it is the creation of incredible experiences that ensures you're in, as the saying goes, the right place at the right time.

The moment of truth isn't anything new in business. In September 2005, the *Wall Street Journal*[2] published a story on Procter and Gamble's (P&G) controversial approach known as the *First Moment of Truth* (FMOT). FMOT refers to the incredibly short but crucial window of the three to seven seconds after a shopper first encounters a product on a store shelf. It is in these precious moments that P&G believes that marketers must focus efforts on converting shoppers into customers. To do so takes appealing to their senses, values, and emotions. It's a lot to accomplish in just seconds, but it can be more impactful than the millions of dollars invested in mass advertising aimed at generating awareness and creating preference.

P&G didn't stop there, however. The pioneering brand also looked at what it referred to as the *Second Moment of Truth*. This is, in my opinion, the future of everything as this second moment is defined by the experience a customer has with a product. In Kevin Roberts' book *Lovemarks*, P&G's CEO A. G. Lafley explained the importance of these first and second touch points:

> " The best brands consistently win two moments of truth. The first moment occurs at the store shelf, when a consumer decides whether to buy one brand or another. The second occurs at home, when she uses the brand—and is delighted or isn't. "

In early 2012, Google published an exceptional ebook, *ZMOT: Winning the Zero Moment of Truth*,[3] written by Jim Lecinski, which continued to explore new touch points or moments of truth. Google outlined a three-step model for marketing: stimulus, FMOT, and Second Moment of Truth (SMOT).

In the book, Google and Lecinski identify a critical step between the initial stimulus or the Cluster Funnel stage of "Persuasion" and the P&G's FMOT or the Hook.

Whereas P&G's FMOT focused on in-store, in-the-moment engagement, this ebook introduced the concept of the Zero Moment of Truth (ZMOT)—the few moments before people buy, where impressions are formed and the path to purchase begins. The idea isn't new, but ZMOT can be adapted to the new world of technology and the networks where awareness and influence unfold. ZMOT, as the ebook states, "is that moment when you grab your laptop, mobile phone, or some other wired device and start learning about a product or service (or potential boyfriend) you're thinking about trying or buying."

In other words, consumers will "Google it" (whatever is important for you to learn more about) and that's where FMOT begins. In addition to Googling, they're going to tweet, Facebook, YouTube, Pinterest, and so on, their search until they either get information or conversations about the product or service they are searching for.

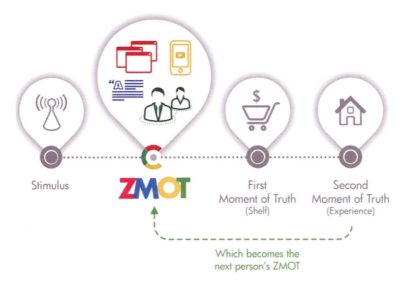

Stimulus     **ZMOT**     First Moment of Truth (Shelf)     Second Moment of Truth (Experience)

Which becomes the next person's ZMOT

As the ebook points out, 79 percent of consumers say they use a smart phone to help with shopping. In addition, 70 percent of Americans look at product reviews before making a purchase. *If 70 percent of consumers pick up a laptop, tablet, smart phone, or another connected device to learn more about your product or business after initial contact, what is it that they find?*

The decision makers in your organizations might think that you're doing everything you need to. After all, you have a website, right? You have accounts on Facebook, Twitter, YouTube, and Pinterest . . . FTW (for the win)! But to the person who's connected not only digitally but socially, today's online presences are just pages with a lot of marketing text or videos.

The dynamic customer is just that . . . dynamic. Static pages, commercials, or walls rich with trivial conversations and promotions are not going to guide consumers or B2B customers from ZMOT to FMOT. They need substance, personalization, and shared experiences to help guide them to the next step . . . to help them complete their journey.

Diving deeper into Google's ZMOT, it expands the customer journey by connecting the Second Moment of Truth or "the experience" with among the most influential of steps, the Ultimate Moment of Truth. The UMOT as I call it is the influence loop that connects back to the Zero Moment of Truth for connected customers. It is these shared experiences that influence impressions and decisions when someone searches or asks for information.

When someone searches, it's often that the shared experiences of those who've already completed the journey will influence the moments of truth for those seeking direction. While that may seem esoteric or perhaps commonsensical, the shared experiences of others can be designed. And for the most part, they aren't today. No matter how brilliant your product design, the list of features, the number of apps you've introduced, or the creative genius behind your marketing, advertising, and social media campaigns, the ultimate moment of truth, what people will actually say about your product, is more aspirational in design than intentional.

Shared experiences are the natural result or byproduct of product design. They either provide an exceptional, shareable experience or they don't. Customers are either delighted or they're not. If experiences aren't engineered to contribute back to the Zero Moment of Truth, they are by default left to chance. Customers will then share whatever it is they encounter because that moment is left for them to define instead of you. And with the pervasiveness and accessibility of new media, that experience is going to be shared. As Jeff Bezos once famously said, "Your brand is what people say about you when you're not in the room." The bottom line is, it's time to think about the experience we want people to have and share and then use new digital channels to steer each step along the journey to win in each moment of truth.

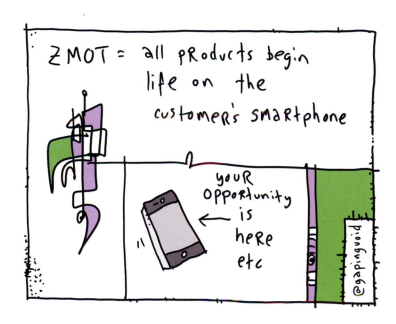

CHAPTER

7

# THE ULTIMATE MOMENT OF TRUTH

We should come home from adventures, and perils, and discoveries every day with new experience and character.

—Henry David Thoreau

Did you know that consumers rely on 10 or more sources in making purchase decisions? Between 2010 and 2011 the average number of sources used not only doubled, but new technologies emerged to facilitate discovery and engagement around these sources.

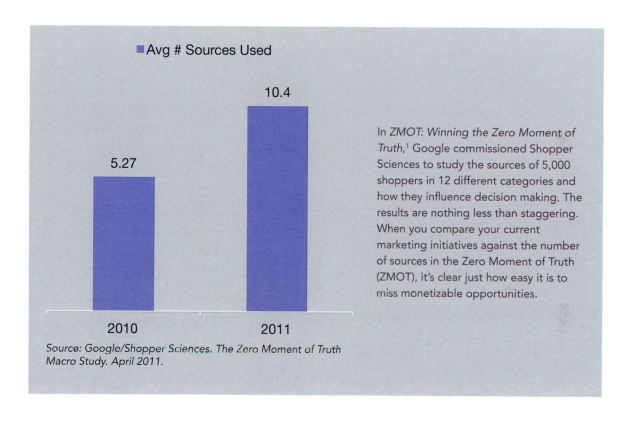

**Avg # Sources Used**

10.4

5.27

2010    2011

*Source: Google/Shopper Sciences. The Zero Moment of Truth Macro Study. April 2011.*

In *ZMOT: Winning the Zero Moment of Truth*,[1] Google commissioned Shopper Sciences to study the sources of 5,000 shoppers in 12 different categories and how they influence decision making. The results are nothing less than staggering. When you compare your current marketing initiatives against the number of sources in the Zero Moment of Truth (ZMOT), it's clear just how easy it is to miss monetizable opportunities.

| Category Purchased | Number of sources used by the typical shopper | Average usage across sources | % of shoppers influenced at ZMOT |
| --- | --- | --- | --- |
| Automotive | 18.2 | 34% | 97% |
| Technology (Consumer Electronics) | 14.8 | 30% | 92% |
| Voters | 14.7 | 35% | 95% |
| Travel | 10.2 | 22% | 99% |
| Over-the-Counter Health | 9.8 | 18% | 78% |
| Consumer Packaged Goods: Grocery | 7.3 | 15% | 61% |
| Consumer Packaged Goods: Health/Beauty/Personal Care | 7 | 14% | 63% |
| Quick-Serve Restaurant | 5.8 | 12% | 72% |
| Banking | 10.8 | 25% | 91% |
| Insurance | 11.7 | 26% | 94% |
| Credit Card | 8.6 | 19% | 81% |
| Investments | 8.9 | 20% | 89% |

*Source: Google/Shopper Sciences. Zero Moment of Truth Macro Study. U.S. April 2011.*

Even something as simple as researching quick-serve restaurants involves an average of 5.8 sources. Shopping for a car? Well, that shoots up to an average of 18.2 sources. It's not just B2C, though. People in every industry imaginable from B2B to politics to education are searching for information to help them make better decisions. Voters, on average, will touch 14.7 sources before voting. For the record, that's just below the 14.8 average number of sources that people said they use to shop for electronics.

Average # of Sources Used by Category

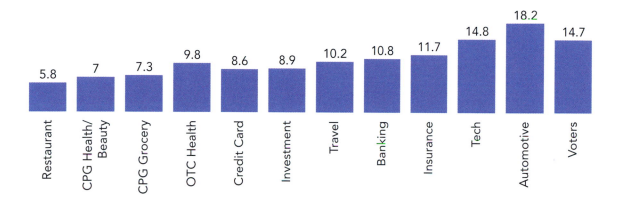

| Restaurant | CPG Health/Beauty | CPG Grocery | OTC Health | Credit Card | Investment | Travel | Banking | Insurance | Tech | Automotive | Voters |
|---|---|---|---|---|---|---|---|---|---|---|---|
| 5.8 | 7 | 7.3 | 9.8 | 8.6 | 8.9 | 10.2 | 10.8 | 11.7 | 14.8 | 18.2 | 14.7 |

**Q2: When you were considering purchasing [PRODUCT], what sources of information did you seek out to help with your decision?**
**Base: *N* = 5,003**

*Source: Google/Shopper Sciences. The Zero Moment of Truth Macro Study. April 2011.*

In an increasingly social and mobile world, the ability to influence decisions reaches beyond search, in-store, and traditional media. While traditional media's influence is trending downward, not surprisingly, mobile and social are trending upward. Yet, if you look at most marketing budgets today, company spending doesn't match consumer behavior. Yes, money is invested in social media, mobile apps, search, online marketing, and so on, but investments in creating amazing experiences in each is disproportionate to the level of influence these channels carry.

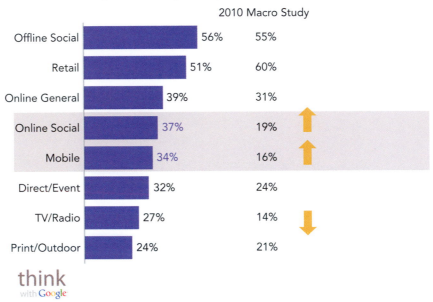

### Social and mobile are growing significantly in influence compared to a year ago

| | | 2010 Macro Study |
|---|---|---|
| Offline Social | 56% | 55% |
| Retail | 51% | 60% |
| Online General | 39% | 31% |
| Online Social | 37% | 19% |
| Mobile | 34% | 16% |
| Direct/Event | 32% | 24% |
| TV/Radio | 27% | 14% |
| Print/Outdoor | 24% | 21% |

think
with Google

**Q5: We'd like you to tell us how influential each of these sources of information was to you at the time. Please select a number from 1 to 10 for each of the sources, where 1 is "least influential" and 10 is "most influential."**

*Source: Google/Shopper Sciences. The Zero Moment of Truth Macro Study. April 2011.*

Let's take a look at apparel shoppers for a moment. Not only do consumers rely on multiple sources offline and online to make decisions, they use multiple devices to do so. PCs, tablets, and smart phones are real-time windows into a real-time world. And each window requires a dedicated and optimized design. Each design must contribute to a holistic experience across channels. The experience requires clear definition and thought-out design.

Apparel shoppers research across multiple devices:
More than 1 in 5 use tablets or mobile devices on **a daily basis** for shopping.

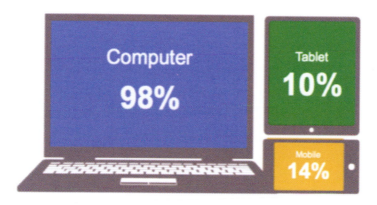

*Source: GoogleComplete. "The Role of Mobile and Video in the Apparel Shopper Digital Path to Purchase." July 2012.*

Consumer dependence on social and mobile will only continue to rise as the influence of traditional media wanes. The opportunities for you to engage consumers grow exponentially. But without study, experimentation, and investment, what might have been missed opportunities then become opportunity costs. Essentially, by not investing in creating experiences in these new channels of influence, you are by default participating in Digital Darwinism, where technology and society are advancing faster than businesses can adapt.

We cannot appreciate the extent of our efforts to engage customers differently if we cannot appreciate the extent of the real opportunity before us.

# THE ULTIMATE MOMENT OF TRUTH

The Ultimate Moment of Truth (UMOT) represents the experience that people share after using your product and engaging with your company over time. Blog posts, YouTube videos, reviews, each in their own way direct people to take their next steps accordingly. When we talk about the idea of experience, it's not only in reference to User Experience (UX) or Customer Experience, it's also about Information Experience . . . what's shared, what comes back, what people are sharing about those experiences. Like SEO (Search Engine Optimization), these moments can be predetermined and optimized.

Your website isn't enough.

You might think that because you have a presence on Facebook, Google+, Twitter, YouTube, Pinterest, that you're doing what you need to. But, you're not.

The future of influence lies in experience. The experiences people have with your product, your company, your representatives, define the brand through the expressions they share.

## Your work must focus on expressions, not impressions.

The connected consumer values information from friends, reviews, and shared experiences ahead of what you publish on your site. Therefore, as you think about strategy and the balance of channels and the overall marketing mix, add one additional element to the equation . . . defining the experiences you want felt in the Second Moment of Truth (SMOT) and shared

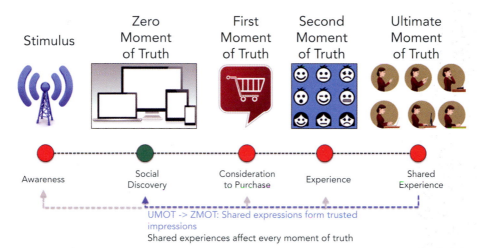

Source: www.shutterstock.com.

in the Ultimate Moment of Truth. The first contributes to satisfaction, bond, and loyalty. The second is an investment in generating word of mouth, advocacy, and influence.

1. **ZMOT**—It's what people search and find after encountering the stimulus that directs their next steps.

2. **FMOT**—It's what people think when they see your product and it's the impressions they form when they read the words describing your product.

3. **SMOT**—It's what people feel, think, see, hear, touch, smell, and (sometimes) taste as they experience your product over time. It's also how your company supports them in their efforts throughout the relationship.

4. **UMOT**—It's that shared moment at every step of the experience that becomes the next person's Zero Moment of Truth (ZMOT).

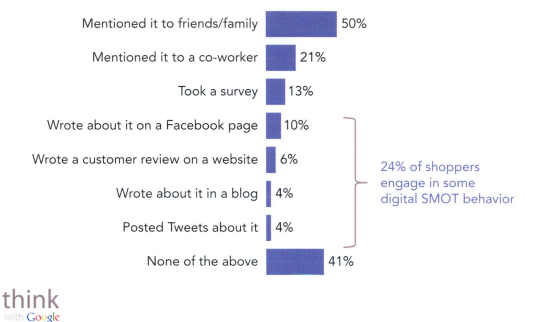

| Activity | Percentage |
|---|---|
| Mentioned it to friends/family | 50% |
| Mentioned it to a co-worker | 21% |
| Took a survey | 13% |
| Wrote about it on a Facebook page | 10% |
| Wrote a customer review on a website | 6% |
| Wrote about it in a blog | 4% |
| Posted Tweets about it | 4% |
| None of the above | 41% |

24% of shoppers engage in some digital SMOT behavior

**Q7: After buying [PRODUCT], which of these activities did you do to share your experience?**
**Base: *N* = 5,003**

*Source: Google/Shopper Sciences. The Zero Moment of Truth Macro Study. April 2011.*

People are going to talk, so give them something to talk about. That's the opportunity you have if you focus on creating experiences. Whether they're good or bad, they're shared. And we're only at the beginning. Your connected customer is increasingly taking to networks and forums to voice their experiences. Knowing that these numbers are growing, especially in digital channels, what do you want them to experience? What do you want them to share? Someone must take responsibility for designing and defining the experience.

That's where you come in.

Understanding the new customer journey is the only way to see what it is we don't know we're missing. Not sure where to start? Walk a day in the life of your connected customers and discover the touch points and sources that influence them. You must also understand how your business performs in these moments of truth to learn how to improve and optimize discoverability and ultimately the experiences people feel and share.

## Now let's embark on the dynamic customer journey to:

**1.** Learn

**2.** Adapt

**3.** Optimize

**4.** Define the experience

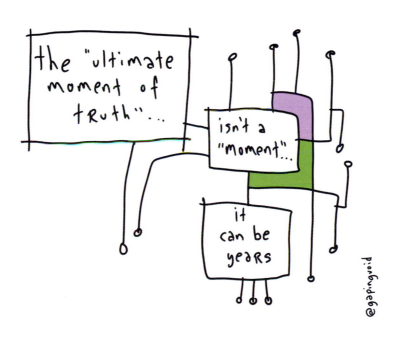

CHAPTER

# [ OPENING A WINDOW INTO NEW CONSUMERISM ]

It is good to learn what to avoid by studying the misfortunes of others.

—Publius Syrius

Consumers are more informed than ever before. From the Zero Moment of Truth to the Ultimate Moment of Truth, consumers are taking control of their journey, discovering relevant information and making decisions their way in real time. To what extent are connected customers disrupting the current market and how fast will this grow over time? The answer is different for each business. But, the answer is there to uncover nonetheless. You just have to do the research. That's where everything begins.

## See, without analysis:

- There can be no insights.
- Without insights, relevant and meaningful strategies are elusive.
- Without strategy, there can be no return on investment (ROI).[1]

Behavior of connected consumers is not only changing, it's opening and closing traditional touch points, places, and ways to engage customers in real time and at the right time. And customer expectations have changed the locks to the doors that open new channels of engagement. To unlock them takes more than showing up and knocking. It certainly doesn't take a locksmith or a battering ram either. It takes understanding, participating, and having a genuine intention to earn relevance. These technologies then become two-way channels for learning and engagement.

To create experiences requires first defining what that experience will look like. Opening a window into new consumerism and taking in the splendor and magnitude of your customer landscape will also reveal the behavior and expressions that result from the experiences you create and those that are created for you. What we're looking for here are the paths where experiences are shared and how they define or alter the direction of people in the moments of truth.

# [ DISCOVERY DISRUPTED ]

Consumers have access to valuable information that is available on demand whenever and wherever. Conversations with trusted sources can take place in real time. As a result, consumers have become enterprising and elusive. Relying on SEO, social media engagement, websites, advertising, in-store visibility, and every form of traditional marketing in play is no longer enough.

For the foreseeable future your business will be in a state of disruption. You may need to operate outside your comfort zones to reach a customer who is in fact divided into three distinct behavior types.

# OPENING THE DOOR TO A NEW GENERATION OF CONNECTED CONSUMERISM

While writing *The End of Business as Usual,* I uncovered three different sets of customer behavior patterns in the decision-making journey: traditional, digital, and connected. Although there is some crossover between traditional and digital and increasingly digital and connected, the latter is much more dynamic. Even though we're focusing here on the connected customer, let's review quickly the three groups to help give you a clear picture:

1. **Traditional**—Influenced by traditional advertisements in print, online, and over the air/cable. Reliant on word of mouth among people they know and trust in the real world. Email and websites form the bridge between traditional and digital.

2. **Digital**—Lives online, but enjoys traditional media as well. Decisions begin by searching Google. Information is collected by visiting websites and review communities. The bridge shared between digital and connected is represented by Facebook, YouTube, Pinterest, and other popular social networks and mobile apps.

3. **Connected**—This is Generation C . . . the connected. The most mobile of the bunch, connected customers live online through a portable device for the majority of the time. From smart phones to tablets to laptops, their smaller window into the world is much more real time and provides them with what could be argued as a much bigger picture. They scan bar codes in stores to compare prices and read reviews. Connected customers contribute actively to reviews on multiple sites and readily share experiences in social

networks. They blog and publish videos sharing every stage of experiences pre-, mid-, and posttransaction. QR codes (quick response codes) to them are often a disappointment, as once they're scanned, they only lead to a website (that often won't load well on a mobile device).

Connected consumers are empowered, informed, and demanding. They are comfortable sharing more than you realize and will share with you if they feel there's value in return. If they Like you on Facebook or follow you on Twitter, they don't expect editorial programming or entertainment as much as they do a sense of exclusivity, privilege, and access to special offers not available anywhere else. Gen C'ers are also driving social and mobile commerce. They shop socially, albeit virtually, and want to pay via mobile. That's their window to the world. Here's the key takeaway: *They not only make decisions differently, they influence and are influenced differently. New touch points are springing up in each moment of truth every day. Your connected customers aren't only becoming more demanding, but also discerning. Their expectations are permanently changing the way you engage them.*

**Follow these four steps to connect with the connected customer:**

**1.** Listen

**2.** Learn

**3.** Engage

**4.** Adapt

Without understanding how your customers behave, you cannot legitimately design a desired experience. Without knowing their expectations, you cannot exceed them.

Knowing this, your next steps are to compare your customer activity, apply it to one of these three groups, and then assess how your current marketing, sales, and service strategies optimize the experiences for each. While we're on the subject, do you know what the *experience* of your brand or business is for each group and do you know what it is about their experiences that they're sharing?

# OPENING THE WINDOWS TO DIGITAL INFLUENCE

Understanding the connected consumer is the only way to develop meaningful marketing, sales, and service strategies. What's more is that doing so also inspires a vision for what their experience could be and therefore requires you to formulate what you want that experience to be. Without this, the experience is left to the customer to determine and share. This creates chaos and confusion in the market.

What does your brand stand for—not just today, but also for the connected, discerning, and elusive customer of the future?

It's time to get in front of transformation instead of reacting to it. The only way to do that is to realize that the customer you think you know and the customer you need to know are not the same person.

Let's start with word of mouth. We know it's important. We know that what people see, think, say, and share influences the impressions and actions of others. But, do we know to what extent it impacts our business? Do we realize where and when this is happening today? And most important, do we know how to proactively increase this activity to desired results?

Capturing this information will help you prioritize channel strategies and stories. Additionally, it will surface opportunities to where and how to create value, address expectations, and steer activity to the benefit of your business and the customer experience.

Crowdtap, a company that helps businesses run influence marketing initiatives, published a friendly infographic and accompanying report to visualize the impact of digital word of mouth.[2] I dissected the graphic to zero in on why you should learn more about how influence can help your marketing, branding, and sales efforts.

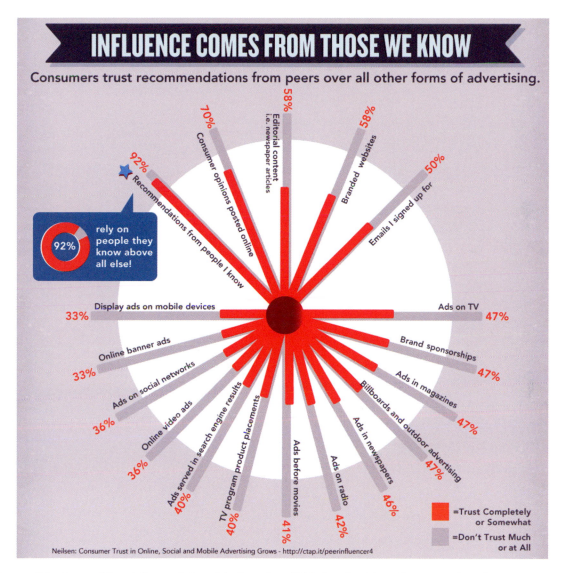

# INFLUENCE COMES FROM THOSE WE KNOW

Consumers trust recommendations from peers over all other forms of advertising.

92% rely on people they know above all else!

Recommendations from people I know — 92%
Consumer opinions posted online — 70%
Editorial content i.e. newspaper articles — 58%
Branded websites — 58%
Emails I signed up for — 50%
Ads on TV — 47%
Brand sponsorships — 47%
Ads in magazines — 47%
Billboards and outdoor advertising — 47%
Ads in newspapers — 46%
Ads on radio — 42%
Ads before movies — 41%
TV program product placements — 40%
Ads served in search engine results — 40%
Online video ads — 36%
Ads on social networks — 36%
Online banner ads — 33%
Display ads on mobile devices — 33%

= Trust Completely or Somewhat
= Don't Trust Much or at All

Neilsen: Consumer Trust in Online, Social and Mobile Advertising Grows - http://ctap.it/peerinfluencer4

Source: "The Power of Peer Influence," Copyright Crowdtap, 2012; download the whitepaper at http://corp.crowdtap.com.

## PEER RECOMMENDATIONS DRIVE SALES

Crowdtap polled 1,000 men and women asking what has influenced them to purchase a new product in the past three months:

**70%**  A friend or family member suggested it online

**61%**  A friend or family member suggested it to me in person or by phone

**59%**  I read about it online in an article

**49%**  I learned about it in an advertisement (magazine/TV/radio/online ad)

**32%**  Someone I follow but don't know or barely know mentioned it online

Crowdtap Poll - http://ctap.it/peerinfluencer5

Source: "The Power of Peer Influence," Copyright Crowdtap, 2012; download the whitepaper at http://corp.crowdtap.com.

Here, Crowdtap polled 1,000 people to share how they were influenced to make a purchase in the past three months. Not surprisingly but certainly revealing, 92 percent claimed that they were influenced by people they know. Have you ever posted or read a review of a product or business online? You're not alone. Seventy percent stated that shared opinions online affected purchase decisions.

To break it down a bit more, Crowdtap looked at each medium to provide insight into what marketing efforts we may want to prioritize. Of the 1,000 surveyed, 70 percent were influenced online. Second, at 61 percent, word of mouth was still a significant influence, but in a different form—either in person or by phone. Third, reading an article online influenced 59 percent of consumer purchases. Think about the growing role blogs, reviews, and YouTube videos will play here.

Digital influence is expanding beyond the boundaries of digital screens, impacting business decisions online and offline. The real-time web is moving faster each day. Your job is to help your business move faster than real time to define and lead experiences.

As you read this, decisions are made for or against you. In the next chapter, we examine the dynamic customer journey and the new touch points that are equally becoming consumer-powered platforms for shared experiences.

CHAPTER

9

# THE DYNAMIC CUSTOMER JOURNEY

All experience is an arch to build upon.

—Henry Brooks Adams

Engagement is as much art as it is science. Understanding the behavior of your connected consumer takes practice of the social sciences—from digital anthropology and psychology to sociology and ethnography. Behavior exposes patterns in consumer activity with these new touch points and resources. Appreciating how customers form opinions and make decisions inspires empathy and creativity. This research can be summed up in the concept of the decision ellipse or what my colleagues and I at Altimeter Group refer to as the *Dynamic Customer Journey*.[1]

What you'll learn from researching what consumers are doing online is, well . . . everything. Most notably, your business will now gain clarity in how and where to focus efforts in order to shape decisions and experiences pre-, during, and postcommerce. Said another way, you'll gain insight into each moment of truth. Additionally, you'll learn the specific factors, people, technologies, communities, and resources that affect each stage of your customer's journey. The results will contribute to a far more accurate point of view that tailors marketing, sales, service, and loyalty strategies to be more effective and engaging. But it won't stop there.[2]

Inspired by McKinsey's work and my own research, I set out to reimagine the traditional sales funnel into a constant and very public elliptical path that often repeats itself.[3] Not only is it constant, every shared experience and touch point influences the decisions of all those who enter the decision ellipse. Experiences are now everything. For if you don't define or shape experiences proactively, your brand is left for others to create in the Ultimate Moment of Truth.

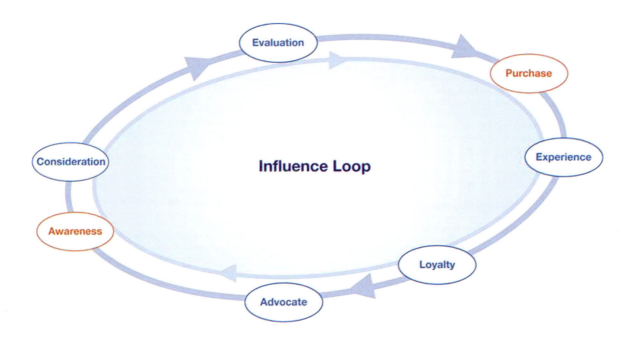

On the surface, the stages of the DCJ reflect similar methodologies to the sales funnel, but the DCJ is designed to uniquely capture the path of your connected customer.

The AIDA funnel implies that customers move along a linear path from Attention to Interest to Decision to Action; and loyalty and advocacy are often assumed to be a by-product following each transaction. Research already shows that connected customers move into a state of neutrality, which can tilt toward negative or positive.

**Each step is unique in the contributing factors for how consumers discover, analyze, choose, and share. Think about the moments of truth here and what people search for, say, share, experience, and what channels affect each of the following steps within the DCJ:**

1. Awareness

2. Consideration

3. Evaluation

4. Purchase

5. Experience

6. Loyalty

7. Advocacy

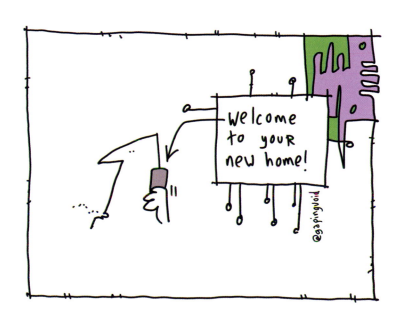

Whether through traditional or social search, asking questions within one's social graph, or simply reading reviews, shared experiences, whether good or bad, affect the next steps of all connected customers that follow. The truth is that before customers can even think about becoming loyal or an advocate for your business, they must first experience the journey once again to validate their decision. If anything comes up different from the first, they may consider new alternatives. Either way, the entire journey is very social and very public. Customers are more connected and informed than ever before and it is the Ultimate Moment of Truth that defines the journey for all connected customers who take passage.

Not only is the journey elliptical, at the center of the DCJ is the influence loop—fed by the Ultimate Moments of Truth. Shared experiences are fed into the loop, forever indexed, and extracted during the moments of truth consumers experience.

# The importance of the influence loop cannot be overstated. It affects every stage of the journey, every moment of truth.

The screens your connected customers use to search and purchase, the people who influence them, the content that informs them, the social networks they rely on, the collective experiences of others, and the real-time conversations that shape impressions, each introduce guidance, doubt, and validation that can work for you or against you. At every stage of the DCJ consumers can share experiences that feed into a discoverable online repository that influences all those who embark on a similar journey. Without content or conversations that offer positive experiences at each step, there can be no hope for preference or a decision in your favor. And, without positive experiences there is no opportunity to establish customer loyalty or advocacy.

The dynamic customer journey is among the most important steps in the discovery process. My work at Altimeter Group has further validated this research and its importance in both making the case for digital transformation and for developing targeted and meaningful strategies.

Together with Charlene Li, Alan Weber, Rebecca Lieb, Susan Etlinger, and Jeremiah Owyang, we've researched what this journey looks like for financial institutions, biopharmaceutical companies, insurance providers, government organizations, auto manufacturers, fashion brands, and everything in between. During my research for my previous book, I also studied the DCJ's dimensions with small and local businesses. While the touch points and sources of influence change, there are consistencies throughout everyone's journey. But the point is that the journey is constantly evolving and revealing.

When it comes to which side of the dollar you wish to be on, walking through DCJ answers that question each and every time . . . over time. It helps you to prioritize investments in technology networks and platforms at every stage of the journey—through every moment of truth. It reveals which experiences are shared, where experiences fall apart. It introduces who influences one another where and what happens next. It opens the door to networks of relevance during each stage of the decision-making cycle.

CHAPTER

10

# INSIDE THE ELLIPSE: EMBARKING ON THE DYNAMIC CUSTOMER JOURNEY

We do not see things as they are. We see them as we are.

— The Talmud

To define the dynamic customer journey (DCJ) in a way that's meaningful, advantageous, and shareable for your organization and your customers you'll need to open your mind, your heart, and your imagination.[1]

It is only by walking in the digital footsteps of your customers that you can uncover a new landscape of opportunities for engagement, as well as a new reality for your business. Embracing your connected customers will help them embrace you in return. At a minimum, the gifts you receive by embarking on this journey and investing in engagement, education, and meaningful experiences are empathy, relevance, and ultimately reciprocity—all of which are measurable by traditional business metrics.

It's time to define the experience where the product brings that experience to life and the technologies you employ contribute to that experience. You are the new CEO . . . the chief experience officer.

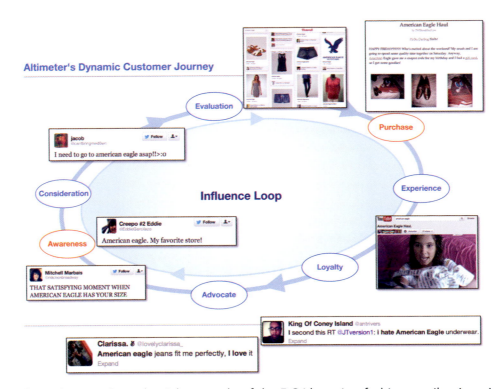

Altimeter's Dynamic Customer Journey

Walking through a simple and quick example of the DCJ by using fashion retailer American Eagle as an example, you can identify and organize shared experiences across various social networks into various moments of truth. As Gen C takes to search engines and status updates to research, ask and answer questions, and share experiences, several opportunities present themselves for businesses to listen, learn, engage, and adapt.

1.  Listen to how people communicate following various stimuli, messages, and new information sources to learn how customers are guided to take their next steps from awareness to consideration and evaluations (the Zero Moment of Truth).

2.  Learn how customer journeys unfold based on the information that comes back in their discovery process. Who are the experts? What are the communities where people go? Who influences them? What do they find and learn? What technologies and services do they use? What happens as a result?

**3** Engage customers in each moment of truth based on their expectations and the opportunities presented to provide value or resources.

**4** Adapt processes, strategies, and technology investments to improve steps 1 to 3.

As you'll soon see, the dynamic customer journey presents moments of truth that either lead people to you or away from you. Each moment is yours to define. The journey is rich with data, relevant networks, influential authorities and peers, and also technology sources.

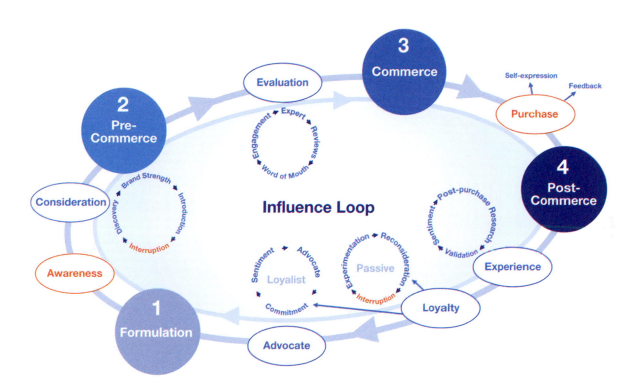

To help you make sense of the DCJ in your work, let's look at each stage at a high level.

# FORMULATION (STIMULUS)

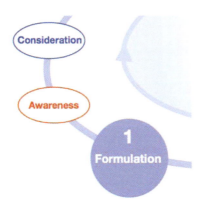

Without awareness of an option there can be no consideration of choosing it. Every touch point is open to disruption directly and indirectly. The effectiveness of your marketing, whether a derivative of paid, earned, or owned media, represents a trigger that sparks the dynamic customer journey for connected customers. What's different now are the channels, techniques, and times your messages can reach people.

The question for you to answer is how you can use new media to stimulate awareness and consideration in ways that complement the customer journey.

## ROLE MODEL: TOMS

TOMS Shoes partnered with 8thBridge to spread the word about its One for One movement while promoting social commerce in the news feed. Using Facebook's Open Graph, "Shoppable Stories" let consumers click "Want," "Love," or "Own" on TOMS ecommerce site, which sends an update to Facebook, allowing friends to do the same within the news feed. This stimulus introduces TOMS into the streams of individuals using friends as the marketing medium and relationships as the currency.

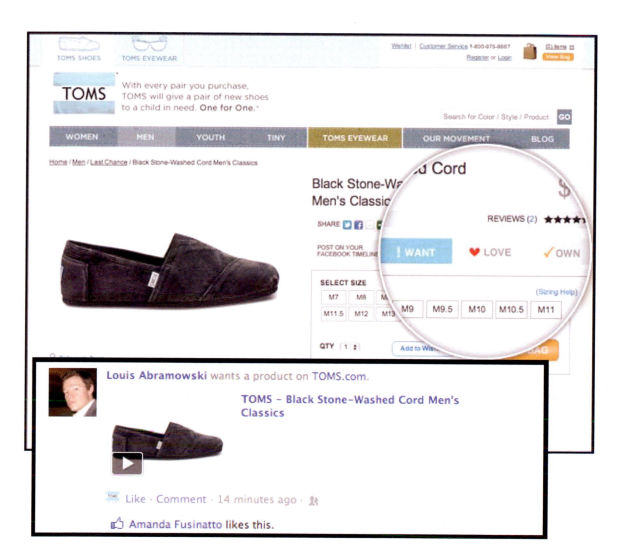

# PRECOMMERCE (ZERO MOMENT OF TRUTH)

Purchases are researched, influenced by social proof, or impulse driven. Your business must contribute to the exchange, research, and discovery process to drive resulting actions.

Here, stimuli trigger the act of search and conversations to learn more about businesses or brands. In the Zero Moment of Truth, your brand presence and discoverability are tested. The stimulus, whether created by you or your competition, reveals information about your product or service and that of others. The strength of your brand, the quality of results to every search query in every network, the words people use as they answer questions or share experiences, and the caliber of reviews in every network determine your customer's next steps and the fate of your organization in the decision-making cycle.

What people hear and say in the Zero Moment of Truth (ZMOT) first requires understanding and then definition. What comes back in the ZMOT should not be left to chance. The journey is far more complex than the funnel ever imagined.

See, unlike the traditional funnel where brands are narrowed through research, the number of considerations actually goes up based on what is uncovered through discovery and engagement. It is what is asked, shared, and what comes back that tests your brand's performance in discoverability.

Any business plugged into social listening can uncover in real time opportunities for engagement. This is what's called a *moment of interruption* . . . similar to a common question that's asked on the dance floor, "May I cut in?"

What you say, how, and when contributes to the impression of your prospect and more importantly, what happens next.

The questions you need to answer here and in each step of the journey are: What experiences do you want people to share and what actions do you want to happen next?

In this stage, peers and trusted experts also shape and steer impressions and next steps. Find them. Learn from them. Engage them.

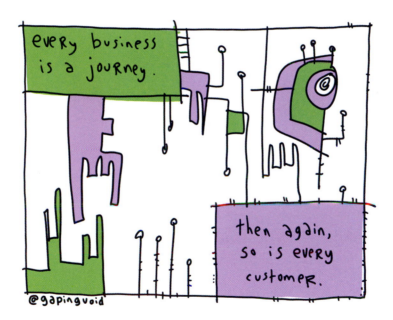

# ROLE MODEL: GIANTNERD

Giantnerd built a social platform that's "Powered by Love" and depends on consumer presence, opinions, wants, and needs. Consumers earn rewards for being social and helping others with decisions. These rewards can then be applied to future purchases.

Randall Weidberg, nerd in charge, believes that consumer engagement helps in the ZMOT and also the Ultimate Moment of Truth (UMOT). Most notably, community interaction improves the overall experience, loyalty, and advocacy as a result. "We want the wisdom of the crowd to help consumers make more educated purchases."

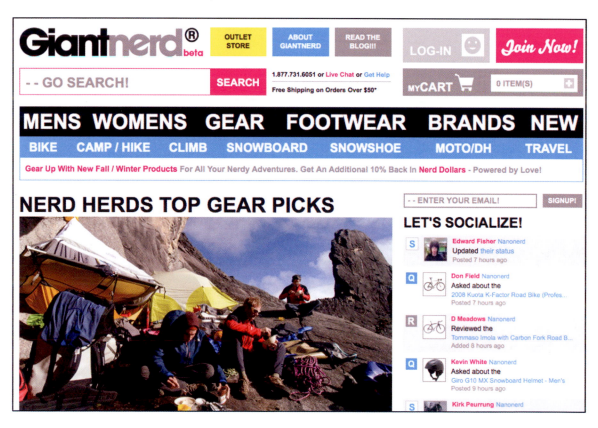

# COMMERCE (FIRST MOMENT OF TRUTH)

As consumers collect information from their trusted sources, they move into a secondary stage of ZMOT and also the First Moment of Truth. They're likely to do one last bit of research before committing to the purchase. Here your product should shine to sway your customer's decision. But again, what comes back in search, in conversations, or through technology contributes to the next steps.

In a retail setting, this is the moment when your customers whip out a mobile device to compare prices, scan a bar code, check their preferred geo-location app, read mobile reviews, and snap and share pictures to send out to the social graph for feedback. The truth is that customers shop for the best deal and advice and they will abandon the transaction if you don't engage—at the right time.

As your customers look at the packaging, talk to representatives or peers, the First Moment of Truth takes over. This is also dubbed the *Amazon moment* where customers compare prices and experiences through their mobile device. Best Buy and Target, among other retailers, are struggling

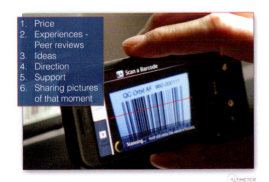

with this moment as customers naturally want to know if the store they are in will match the online price. Technology isn't the only thing that needs to change. Dated policies and processes are also in dire need of updating. When a customer asks if a price can be matched by showing an app or site that lists a lower price, the answer is usually no. Perhaps it's time to revisit that and other policies and technologies that encourage in-the-moment engagement.

The smoother you can make the transaction, the easier it is to ensure that your customers will continue the journey through to the Second and Ultimate Moments of Truth. This isn't just about reducing friction in the information and commerce channels you choose to support. This is about meeting the discerning needs and expectations of your connected customers in the channels and through the screens they prefer. We are indeed becoming a digital society of multitaskers and multiscreeners. As such, you need to invest in a multichannel strategy that appeals to common interests and behavior, which without research is just using new technology because it's in fashion.

The image below visualizes how different age groups use technology to make purchases. Simply by grouping the people who are comfortable or prefer using mobile devices to make purchases, you can justify a dedicated mobile commerce strategy while still investing in traditional and desktop/laptop-based commerce models. Investing in technology and engagement strategies

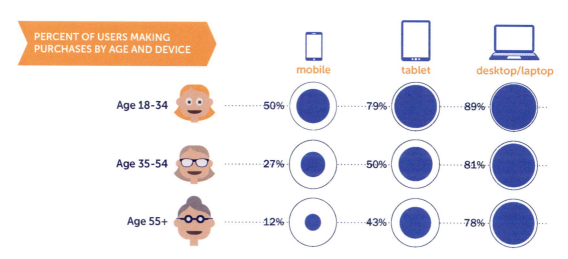

Source: Milo.com, using data from Comscore, eMarketer, Digital Marketing Insights, or Prospr Mobile.

by interest and behavior requires a shift from demographic to psychographic segmentation and targeting.

As you can see, an astounding 50 percent of Millennials are already making purchases on mobile phones, 79 percent are purchasing via tablets, and 89 percent are buying through ecommerce. That's not new. The reality is though that these numbers are moving toward pervasiveness across smaller screens, which require dedicated experiences to be designed. If you compare the numbers on the preceding page to the broader Gen C behavior, you realize that your smart phone and tablet strategy is most likely missing the bigger opportunity. This is about more than creating an app for your business. This is about a distributed yet integrated experience where information and conversations are the conduits to commerce.

Posttransaction, the Second Moment of Truth becomes essential as it fortifies impressions and gives way to the Ultimate Moment of Truth—the experience customers share with others in the influence loop.

# If you think that product experiences are out of your realm of responsibility, think again.

In a postcommerce era where everyone is connected through shared experiences in this dynamic customer journey, your product or service is as much a part of marketing as everything else in your strategy.

In this Second Moment of Truth, the experience that you design is paramount. For if you don't design what it is you want people to feel, think, embrace, and do, that experience will be defined for you.

Striving to improve experiences requires learning how to improve products. Even the almighty Apple tracks feedback and experiences to improve its products and services. Doing so, it realized long ago, not only improves experiences, its better experiences can command a premium.

## CHAPTER 10

# POSTCOMMERCE (ULTIMATE MOMENT OF TRUTH)

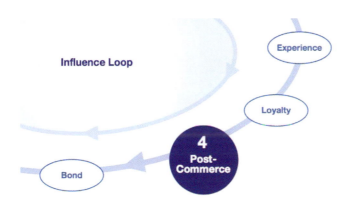

**Influence Loop**

Experience

Loyalty

**4 Post-Commerce**

Bond

The most interesting aspects of the DCJ and either the most beneficial or detrimental to your business, is the Ultimate Moment of Truth. The truth here is that product experiences are broadcast back into the same channels that influenced customers' decisions in the first place, thus becoming part of the influence loop and the Ultimate Moment of Truth.

Consumers will share their experiences, good and bad, now and throughout the lifetime of the product usage. These shared experiences also contribute to the future decisions (ZMOT) of others indefinitely.

Postcommerce experiences contribute to the state of the customer relationship. Great products and services contribute to loyalty. Great engagement inspires advocacy. Underestimating experience says everything about how you value customers. You reap what you sow. Shared experiences, whether good or bad, are what you earn or deserve.

Every day, an increasing number of connected consumers is taking to social networks to ask for help or express sentiment related to business or product-related experiences; some consumers do so to seek resolution from their peers, others broadcast comments as a form of catharsis, and a smaller group of consumers actually hopes to receive a response directly from the company.

The reality is that *social* media is the new normal. A myriad of social networks, whether you use them or not, are now part of the day-to-day digital lifestyle with Facebook, Twitter, Yelp, and YouTube, among others, becoming the places where your customers connect, communicate, and engage around experiences. They take to these social networks and more because they can. The question is: What are you doing about it?

In the Ultimate Moment of Truth, customers are defining the next steps or the ZMOT of others simply by what they contribute in the experience loop.

The importance of defined experiences is just the beginning. It is the investment in a proactive support ecosystem of desirable experiences that not only influence, but reinforce the experience you want people to embrace and, in turn, share.

Businesses will learn to engage in new networks one of two ways: Either businesses will recognize the opportunity to earn relevance through "aha" moments, or they'll say "uh-oh" upon witnessing the impact of a crisis on business, branding, and customer influence when a negative experience goes viral.

**Brands are no longer created; they're co-created.**

The image on the preceding page is a word cloud generated by the tweets of customers who shared their experiences regarding @United (United Airlines). I removed the colorful language as this isn't a discussion about United, but instead how customer experiences are shared and how they influence impressions and decisions. Additionally, this is an example of the necessary examination of how businesses are shaping and reacting to customer experiences in the midst of a digital revolution.

The two words that stand out clearly and represent the importance of our focus over the next several years are . . . *customer service*. If you look closely enough, you'll see two other words surrounding customer service, which symbolize the importance of a renewed or new customer focus . . . *response* and *change*.

In a study published by Maritz Research and evolve24 in 2011,[2] just less than 1,300 consumers were asked about their experiences with Twitter and customer service. As the respondents' ages increased, so did their expectations that companies would read and respond to their experiences.

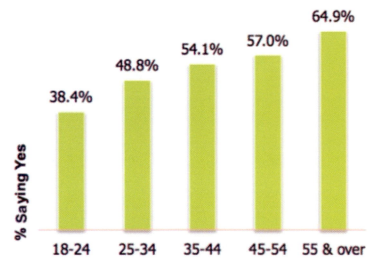

**Do you expect the company to read your tweet?**

% Saying Yes

| 18-24 | 25-34 | 35-44 | 45-54 | 55 & over |
| --- | --- | --- | --- | --- |
| 38.4% | 48.8% | 54.1% | 57.0% | 64.9% |

*Source: Reprinted with permission from IBM.*

Imagine that you are a connected consumer using Twitter to lodge a complaint and get a response that could solve a problem and retain you as a customer, only to be disappointed by the absence of a response. That's exactly what happened to the respondents of the survey. Just over 70 percent said that they did not hear back from a company they reached out to on Twitter. This sets up a bigger problem if the company is in fact on Twitter. It tells consumers that their experience is unimportant and that the business is only present in social networks to market or sell products and not to provide help. Saying nothing to customers with a problem says everything about how you value them.

Providing resolution is only one part of the value proposition. Engagement is defined as the interaction between a brand and a consumer, but it is in how it's measured that counts.

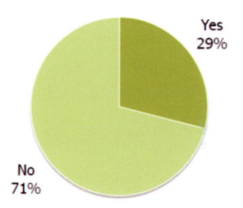

**Has anyone from the company contacted you about your complaint as a result of your tweet?**

Yes 29%

No 71%

*Source: Reprinted with permission from IBM.*

Engagement isn't measured by Likes, comments, impressions, tweets, or retweets. Engagement is measured by the takeaway value, sentiment, and resulting actions following the exchange. People have said that they've felt better once they were contacted by a company representative on Twitter. That says everything. . . .

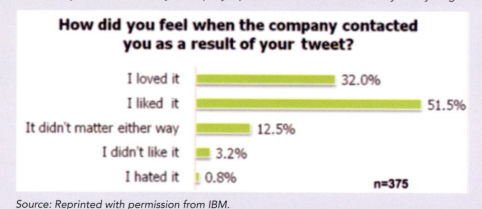

**How did you feel when the company contacted you as a result of your tweet?**

| | |
|---|---|
| I loved it | 32.0% |
| I liked it | 51.5% |
| It didn't matter either way | 12.5% |
| I didn't like it | 3.2% |
| I hated it | 0.8% |

n=375

*Source: Reprinted with permission from IBM.*

Customer service is important. But experiences supersede service. See, without investment in positive experiences, people are forever going to inquire about everything you didn't anticipate.

Let's look at fashion retail for a moment. Conversocial[3] studied customer service responses on Twitter across 10 major U.S. clothing brands. The company found that 50 percent of customer complaints were never answered at all. Of these, 48 percent were customer issues with direct queries to the company; only 9 percent of the tweets were negative comments that criticized companies without really looking for help. We're already missing opportunities to fix, improve, and create *remarkable* experiences.

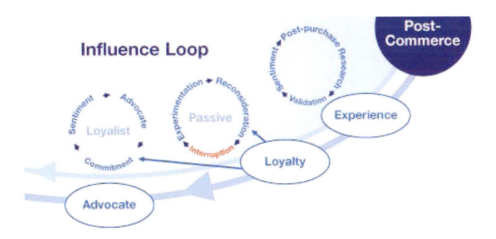

It's not just about online engagement, however. Loyalty and eventually advocacy are driven by what people actually undergo during the Second Moment of Truth and how they translate emotion and experience in the Ultimate Moment of Truth. With connected customers, traditional loyalty or reward programs don't really apply. These programs must be reengineered to ensure an ongoing positive experience and reaffirm customer value posttransaction. So many connected customers—wait, so many customers in *general*—feel that their value to a business ends when the transaction is completed in the commerce stage. Research in the DCJ shows that customers aren't quite *sold* on your product or your brand just because they made the purchase. They run through the ellipse again with the intention of verification, participation, and validation.

Again, direct engagement is key here. Interruption isn't just open to your business; it's open to your competitors to engage your customers as well. Guiding these critical next steps will determine whether your customer abandons ship, becomes a promoter, or far worse, manifests a negative experience that impacts other consumers in the influence loop.

## ROLE MODEL: GIFFGAFF

In working with Lithium,[4] I learned about giffgaff, a "SIM card–only" mobile virtual network operator based in the United Kingdom. Giffgaff is a company that's run by its members. They are rewarded for running parts of the business, such as important functions including sales, marketing, and service. Customers who answer questions in the community, help recruit new members, and promote the company earn rewards. This helps the company to reduce operating costs and it passes the savings back to members. As in the Giantnerd example, customers are wildly supportive of the company as it creates not only a vibrant community but one where they are rewarded for their engagement.

To a giffgaff customer, experiences are everything. If a question or problem arises in the community, it is answered within 90 seconds, 24 hours a day. NPS? Net reputation score? Satisfaction? By investing in proactive experiences and rewarding customers for their engagement, customer satisfaction soared to 90 percent.[5]

The company also launched an Ideas Board, similar to Dell's IdeaStorm and Starbucks's MyStarbucks Idea, to funnel customer engagement and shape the business. To date, giffgaff has received more than 6,000 ideas and more than 50,000 comments, with the company implementing—on average—one member idea every three days.

Imagine that . . . positive experiences are becoming a competitive advantage in a day and age when poor customer engagement and service is unfortunately a commodity.

In the end, transformation isn't easy, but if it were, then providing exceptional customer experiences would become a commodity. This is a time when customers can work for you not just against you. And as customers are demonstrating every day in social and mobile networks, without a thoughtful approach or engagement, every tweet, update, post, video, and interaction is working against you right now. Customer relationships are to be shaped, not simply reacted to or managed. This is why your participation matters now more than ever.

CHAPTER

11

# IMPROVING THE UMOT TO OPTIMIZE THE ZMOT

We must not let go manifest truths because we cannot answer all questions about them.

—Jeremy Collier

Sounds almost playful; it certainly made me smile as I wrote it. But it is a profound topic nonetheless. If there is one thing you take away from this experience, it's that the experiences people share influence the steps other people take and the decisions they ultimately make. No matter how brilliant your marketing efforts, there is no one way to reach your desired audiences nor to create coveted impressions. The power of peer-to-peer influence is perhaps at its greatest potency. Peer-driven word of mouth has always held a powerful relationship between cause and effect. In the 1970s, Fabergé Organics reminded consumers of what's possible when you combine useful products, emotional correlation, and happy customers. The result is shared experiences aka word of mouth, "If you tell two friends about Fabergé Organics shampoo with wheat germ oil and honey, then they'll tell two friends, and so on and so on and so on."[1] While clever marketing, Fabergé's point blank approach is exactly the point. It's not what you say about you, it's what others experience and say about you that counts.

To win in the Moments of Truth, and you have to win in each and every one, apply a simple but important framework to each strategy. But before you do, think of the Moments of Truth much in the same way as you do the funnel. Marketing, service, product development, sales, and so on, must align to not only complement one another but contribute to the experiences of customers from ZMOT to UMOT. Not doing so creates friction internally and externally. Those organizations that reduce friction and enhance experiences win. It's as simple as that. Winning requires a simple framework built upon a solid foundation of internal collaboration: listen, learn, engage, and adapt to enhance and optimize your performance in each Moment of Truth (MOT):

**1** Listen to conversations specific to your customers' discovery process. Walk in their digital footsteps.

**2** Learn how key words, questions, and responses contribute to themes and how those themes evolve.

   **a.** Apply those key words to learn how customers are engaged in ZMOT within social media.

   **b.** Refine your key word strategy based on how people are searching and interacting with one another.

**c.** Apply these insights to SEM (search engine marketing) efforts.

**d.** Also, learn how customers are engaged in ZMOT for search today.

**3** Engage people in the ZMOT and become a respected and appreciated resource to your community.

**a.** Also, engage indirectly by developing a Second Moment of Truth (SMOT)-driven content strategy to win in ZMOT.

    **i.** YouTube videos.

    **ii.** Social-friendly website and/or landing pages.

    **iii.** Utility-driven brand pages in key social networks and communities.

    **iv.** Useful blog posts.

    **v.** Customer reviews and testimonials on social sites.

**b.** Engage customers in the UMOT as well. If there's a problem, fix it. Fix it publicly and rapidly.

    **i.** Create a dedicated role or team to monitor UMOTs in important channels to convert negative experiences into positive outcomes.

**4** Adapt your strategies to improve the discovery journey and how you perform within it. And adapt internally to create frictionless experiences inside and outside the organization.

**a.** Create a path between shared experiences and product innovation and iterations.

**b.** Apply insights inside the organization to rethink roles, rules, and processes and how they can evolve to lead a more beneficial dynamic customer journey.

From ZMOT to FMOT and SMOT to UMOT, shared experiences are the ties that bind decision making. Even though this isn't the 1970s, the old Fabergé commercial still rings true. The difference is that your customer will tell more than two friends and they will tell more than two friends. With access to mobile, social, and the Internet anytime anywhere, friends, experiences, impressions, and expressions are available on demand. As such, there's no need for surprises in what those interactions look like. Yes, make incredible products. Yes, offer helpful sales and fantastic customer support. Market with creativity and vigor. But, also design the types of experiences you want shared in every Moment of Truth. Appreciate the truth for what it is today. Then take control of your fate by not fearing or controlling the truth.

CHAPTER

# THE SIX PILLARS OF SOCIAL COMMERCE

*Understanding the Psychology of Engagement*

The greatest discovery of my generation is that human beings can alter their lives by altering their attitudes of mind.

—William James

Social media is more about social science than technology.[1] As we look at the dynamic customer journey (DCJ) and the moments of truth, we see that the opportunity before us—connected consumerism—is bigger than social media. It's about experience. As such, its value is not realized in the Likenomics[2] of relationship status or in the scores that individuals earn by engaging in social networks.[3]

The value of digital experiences is rooted in people, relationships, and the meaningful actions between them. Yes, it's not just social . . . it's digital and real world experiences that count for everything. The value of branded experiences comes down to the role you play in listening, engaging, and delivering value to customers before, during, and posttransaction. Value is then measured through the exchange of social currencies that contribute to one's capital within each network, including the capital associated with your brand. Through conversations, what we share, and the content we create, consume, and curate, we individually invest in the commerce of information and the relationships that naturally unfold.[4] It is in how these relationships take shape that is both in and out of your control. This is why, in the age of social and mobile networking, relevant engagement and ensuring experiences matter.

# HEAR NO EVIL.
# SEE NO EVIL.
# SPEAK NO EVIL.

Online conversations about you take place even if your organization isn't around to hear it. Some business leaders actually believe that creating a presence in social networks erodes at the control of the brand, risking the consumer governance they've theoretically held onto so triumphantly over the years. If that logic holds, by not engaging in the dynamic customer journey or by sharing only one dimension of your business online, you can control what people think and say online and in each moment of truth.

## However, the truth is that new media did not "invent" conversations, experiences, or opinions.

The control you think you lose by opening up to online engagement actually gives you control. While we are measured by our actions and words, we are also measured by our inaction and silence. Once you understand what people say and don't say, how they connect, what they share, how they discover and make decisions, who influences them, and whom they influence, a blueprint for experiences emerges. Think of it as experience architecture.

People will talk about you whether you are there to hear it or not. The questions you have to answer are: What do you want them to say? What do you want them to do? and What do you want them to feel? Answer these questions and you start to design intentional experiences.

# THE A.R.T. OF ENGAGEMENT

In the dynamic customer journey, the social sciences of psychology, anthropology, communication, economics, human geography, and so on, are essential in building meaningful relationships, guiding relevant experiences, and influencing mutually beneficial behavior. This means that you must first articulate and ultimately design what it is you want the user experience to emulate or evoke.

The concept of social architecture—the A.R.T. of Engagement—is where actions, reactions, and transactions become the fabric of holistic and connected experiences.[5] It's not as easy as deploying campaigns and landing pages. The click path, the outcomes, and the stated value must be optimized, efficient, and worthy of sharing. This is where social science and, in particular, psychology come into play. You must design an experience that captivates the mind or feeds likely emotions to affect desirable behavior in a given context.

# THE PSYCHOLOGY OF SOCIAL COMMERCE

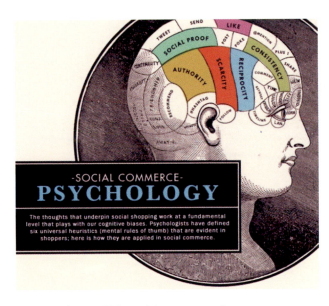

Source: TabJuice, LLC.; socialcommercetoday.com;
blog.squeakywheelmedia.com; interbranddesignforum.com.

The importance of social psychology cannot be overstated. This branch of psychology deals with how people think about influence and how individuals relate to one another. In social networks, the social economy is defined by how people earn and spend social capital. Based on the commerce of actions, words, and intentions (or actions, reactions, and transactions), individuals contribute to their own standing. You earn the relationships and the resulting stature that you deserve.

One day while catching up on the latest news online, I stumbled across a rather interesting infographic developed by TabJuice that creatively communicated the psychology of social commerce. The graphic was inspired by a series of studies based on the work of Robert Cialdini.

The infographic visualized Cialdini's[6] Six Principles of Influence[7] that consumers use to make decisions. Referred to as *thinslicing*, consumers tend to ignore most information available and instead slice off a few relevant information or behavioral cues that are often social to make intuitive decisions.

# HEURISTIC NUMBER 1: SOCIAL PROOF—FOLLOW THE CROWD

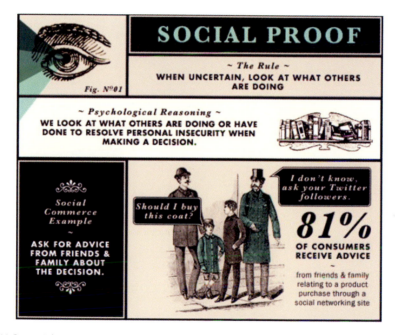

Source: TabJuice, LLC.; socialcommercetoday.com; blog.squeakywheelmedia.com; interbranddesignforum.com.

During the dynamic customer journey, consumers may find themselves at a point of indecision. When consumers are uncertain of what to do next, social proof kicks in to see what others are doing or have done.

To influence decisions, wish lists, popularity lists, social sharing, reviews, and social recommendations become paramount.

# HEURISTIC NUMBER 2:
## AUTHORITY—THE GUIDING LIGHT

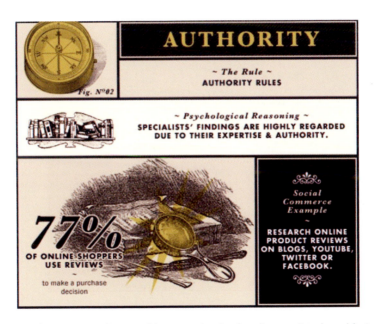

Source: TabJuice, LLC.; socialcommercetoday.com; blog.squeakywheelmedia.com; interbranddesignforum.com.

Authority in social media is not only related to commerce, but it is the very source of how interest graphs take shape. During the dynamic customer journey, authorities guide in effective decision making. Authorities have invested their time, resources, and activity in earning a position of influence, and their reward for doing so is a community of loyalists who place trust in their recommendations.

In Edelman's most recent *Trust Barometer* report, academics and experts topped the list for trust and credibility (66 percent), followed by a technical expert at a company (66 percent).[8]

# HEURISTIC NUMBER 3:
## SCARCITY—LESS IS MORE

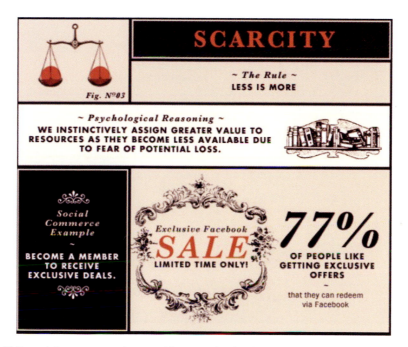

Source: TabJuice, LLC.; socialcommercetoday.com; blog.squeakywheelmedia.com; interbranddesignforum.com.

A function of supply and demand, greater value is assigned to the resources that are, or are perceived to be, less available. Driven by the fear of loss or the stature of self-expression, consumers are driven by the ability to participate as members in exclusive deals. Part affinity, part elitism, consumers have expressed over and over that the ability to have early or select access to offers and promotions is a top reason to connect in social media.

# HEURISTIC NUMBER 4: LIKING—BUILDS BONDS AND TRUST

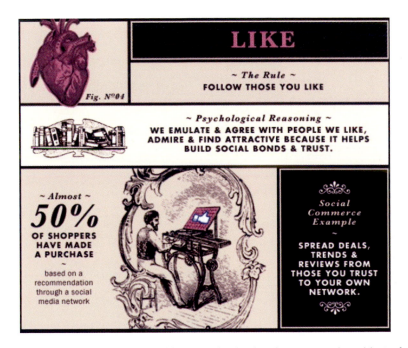

*Source: TabJuice, LLC.; socialcommercetoday.com; blog.squeakywheelmedia.com; interbranddesignforum.com.*

There's an old saying in business: People do business with people they like. That statement is never truer than in social media. Revisiting the Edelman Trust Barometer, the third most trusted person is someone like yourself/peers (65 percent). We have a natural inclination to emulate those we like, admire, and find attractive, because these attributes also contribute to the "guilt by association" impression of self-identity.

# HEURISTIC NUMBER 5:
## CONSISTENCY

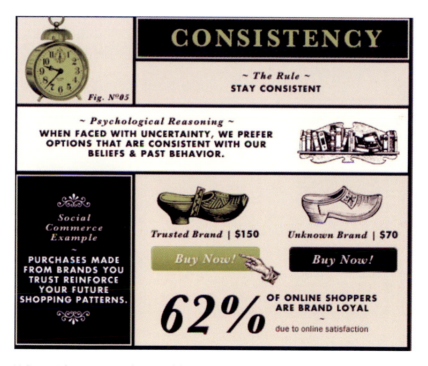

Source: TabJuice, LLC.; socialcommercetoday.com; blog.squeakywheelmedia.com; interbranddesignforum.com.

When faced with uncertainty, consumers tend not to take risks. Rather, they prefer to stay consistent with beliefs or past behavior. When these do not line up in the decision-making cycle, consumers tend to feel cognitive dissonance or true psychological discomfort.

## CHAPTER 12

# HEURISTIC NUMBER 6:
## RECIPROCITY—PAY IT FORWARD

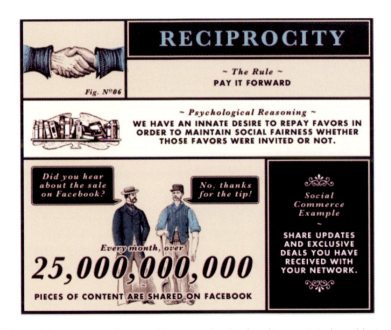

*Source: TabJuice, LLC.; socialcommercetoday.com; blog.squeakywheelmedia.com; interbranddesignforum.com.*

Perhaps the greatest asset in social capital is that of benevolence. It's easy to get caught up in a cycle of paying it backward, where we expect to be paid or rewarded for our goods, services, or actions. However, those who invest in helping others or in paying it forward will earn something greater than a reaction; they will earn a repository of reciprocity. As human beings, we have an innate desire to repay favors to maintain a balance of social fairness whether or not those favors were invited.

# If ignorance is bliss, awareness is awakening.

The psychology of social commerce reveals the emotional elements that activate desirable consumer behavior in each moment of truth throughout the dynamic customer journey. It is the understanding of the six pillars of social commerce that facilitates the development of a more cohesive and connected online experience for customers. More importantly, by investing in the value, productivity, and efficiency of consumer decision making and not just the outcome, businesses can not only earn reciprocity and goodwill, but also earn social capital as a result . . . and that's priceless.

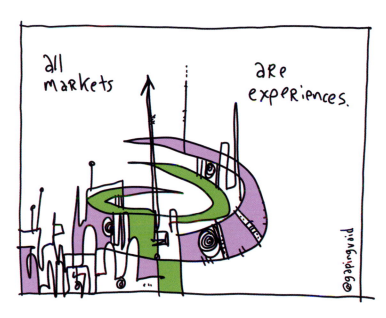

CHAPTER

13

# THE IMPORTANCE OF BRAND IN AN ERA OF DIGITAL DARWINISM

The trouble with learning from experience is that you never graduate.

—Doug Larson attributed,
The Ship of Thought

Now more than ever, what your organization stands for and what it represents can be the foundation for a meaningful competitive advantage. The journey we walked through together in the last several chapters presents a connected customer whose values, personal beliefs, and life experiences combined with personal and professional objectives create the need for personal engagement.

It's not a debate of apathy versus empathy: businesses must align with individuals in order for individuals to stand with businesses. Your organization must go beyond being customer-centric.

Think about the definition of community. The textbook definition of community is a group of people living in the same place or having a particular characteristic in common. At the moment, most businesses do not have an understanding of what a community is and why customers do or do not align with it. Nor does an organization have a singular customer view because the organization is siloed to slice up the customer divisionally, by function and by the desired result. Departments don't talk to one another because they're not measured by collaboration efforts; they're measured by the performance of their function. The traditional funnel no longer works on connected customers. It's far too dynamic and the evolution is spinning the ellipse faster than your business is adapting its vision, mission, and models to react.

The reality is that there isn't a top-down movement to create a singular experience for the customer. As such, there isn't a unified movement within to embrace the customer in something more significant than transactional relationships.

# This has to change.

The future of community requires greater depth of understanding and intention. Community is much more than being a part of something; it's about doing something together that makes being a part of something matter. Community must have a purpose.

To build a true community starts with your vision statement. It is enlivened by your brand. You must define the experience you want people to have with your brand and align that experience with everything that you do. From product development to support to sales and marketing to packaging and presentation to the ethos that fills every hallway, office, and conference room that make up your organization and your brand, you must construct something that's aspirational and worthy of community.

Think of your favorite brand, and the first thing to come to mind is likely a logo, such as the Coca-Cola scripting, a tagline, such as Nike's "Just do it," or a jingle—remember the Oscar Meyer Wiener song? These may be the aspects of a brand you remember, but they are no longer the most important aspects of branding today. Identity, persona, essence, and promise are the new kings and queens of the branding kingdom, thanks to technology and the deeper connections it opens up between brands and consumers.

Markets, consumer behavior, and how businesses connect with customers are all directly impacted by technology.[1] Looking at the rapid erosion of Blockbuster's business model, it's clear to see the impact that technology can have on consumer behavior.[2] During Blockbuster's initial bankruptcy filing, CNBC's *Faber Report* summarized it this way: "At the end of the day, this is one of those bankruptcies that's not really about a financial situation as much as it's about seminal changes in how people ultimately watch video."

The increasingly important role of technology, combined with global economic unrest, means that a company's brand is more important today than it has ever been. Consumers, in search of certainty, rely heavily on a brand's symbolism and significance. We don't have to look much further than Netflix for a recent example of what happens when executives misread the impact of technology and consumer demand and, in turn, make decisions that have negative effects on the business and the brand.

In the case of Netflix and its double whammy of uninformed business decisions, Reed Hastings and company raised prices, which sent customers into an uproar. Feeling the effects of negative sentiment from a full-blown PR crisis and a declining stock price, Netflix then opted to divide the company into two entities: Qwikster would handle DVDs and Netflix would focus on digital and streaming. However, Netflix customers weren't ready for such a bold move in what was largely regarded as an unnecessary direction. The company caved to consumer and investor pressure and folded the two entities back under Netflix, killing off Qwikster as quickly as it had been introduced.

Netflix now must focus on rebuilding its brand to earn and re-earn trust before it can take another aggressive move into the future. Yet, any form of market research that studied conversations in social networks or quite simply, a customer engagement program would have revealed the state of consumer needs in the first place.

Brands that fail to instill a level of confidence in their consumers run the risk of failing. The brands that survive this era of economic disruption will be the ones that are best able to evolve because they recognize the need and opportunity to do so, before their competitors.

# BRANDING IS MORE IMPORTANT THAN EVER BEFORE

In 1984, Apple stunned the world with its now iconic "1984" commercial.[3] It firmly established Apple's brand and ultimately set the stage for the company's significance in the emerging personal computers market. The commercial attained legendary status, but Apple, like every brand, would still need to relentlessly compete for attention and relevance.

A year later, Apple attempted to match its previous success with "Lemmings," a commercial that dramatized the lemming-like behavior of the PC-based work force.[4] The ad, while arguably brilliant, was widely considered a flop, because the image of businesspeople following one another over a cliff confused customers. Over time, Apple's brand slowly degraded, losing touch with its core audience and missing an opportunity to connect with the growing base of consumers seeking personal computers.

When Steve Jobs returned to Apple in 1997, he was on a mission to not only turn around the company he had co-founded, but also to rebrand the company to connect with consumers. In a recently surfaced internal video, Jobs focused on the importance of brand as he introduced the employees to its iconic advertising campaign, "Think Different."[5]

"For me, marketing is about values," said Jobs. "This is a very noisy world and we're not going to get a chance to get people to remember much about us. So, we have to be very clear what we want them to know about us."

The company then looked inward in an attempt to answer the questions: Who is Apple? What does it stand for and where does the brand fit in the world?

66 What we're about isn't making boxes for people to get their jobs done," said Jobs during the company meeting. "Apple's core value is that we believe people with passion can change the world . . . for the better. Those people, crazy enough to think that they can change the world are the ones that actually do. . . . Here's to the crazy ones. 99

The "Think Different" campaign would run from 1997 to 2002 and effectively rebrand Apple for years to come. But that was just one example of how the company would use branding to compete for attention and relevance over the years.

# BRAND EMPATHY: ALWAYS IMPROVE EXPERIENCES

In 2011, Millward Brown Optimor released its annual BrandZ survey that ranked and valued the world's top brands.[6]

Apple surged to the number one spot, soaring 84 percent relative to its 2010 ranking. The company boasts a brand value estimated at $153 billion. Google came in second; however, its brand value fell by 2 percent to $111 billion. IBM came in third, with a 17 percent increase in brand value year over year to tie Google at $111 billion. McDonald's ranked fourth, growing 23 percent and earning a brand value of $81 billion.

Any other company would likely be thrilled to be in fourth place, but not McDonald's. The company is undergoing its most extensive store-by-store makeover in the chain's 56-year history. Gone are the famous yellow and red interior colors. The fiberglass tables and steel chairs have also been removed. McDonald's is adapting to a new era, creating an experience marked by muted colors, wooden tables, and faux leather chairs. And, that's just the beginning. McDonald's is pouring $1 billion into redesigning the consumer experience. The goal is to create an elegant and upscale presence similar to that of Starbucks, Chipotle, and Panera Bread.

As Jim Carras, senior vice president of domestic restaurant development for McDonald's told USA Today, "McDonald's has to change with the times and we have to do so faster than we ever have before."[7]

Meanwhile, don't expect Apple to slow down despite its newly minted, first-place position. Apple will continue to innovate, even as the company mourns the loss of its chief visionary. Expect Apple to continue to inspire meaningful experiences and establish a sense of unparalleled belonging. This is the charge of any brand that wants to stay at the top of the brand value list. In the face of Digital Darwinism, reinvention, constant relevance, and perpetual value become the pillars for an adaptive business.

This begins with embracing a culture of innovation and adaptation—a culture that recognizes the impact of disruptive technology and how consumer preference and affinity are evolving. Social and mobile networks, tablets, smart phones, syndicated commerce, augmented reality, and gamification represent some of the game changers that businesses must either embrace or deeply study to determine bottom line impact. If an organization cannot recognize opportunities to further compete for attention and relevance, it cannot, by default, create meaningful connections or drive shareable experiences. The brand, as a result, will lose preference in the face of consumer choice, which may one day lead to its succumbing to Digital Darwinism.

Perhaps Jobs said it best: "This is a very noisy world . . . So, we have to be very clear what we want them to know about us."

I would just add: "And never stop."

As you think about the experience you wish customers to have before, during, and following transactions, think about what it is they're thinking, feeling, seeing, and touching in every step. This is the experience. Now, what people share in the Ultimate Moment of Truth are the experiences that, in turn, define your brand.

# Give people something to stand with, something to believe in.

A strong community is the net result of something designed to be meaningful and remarkable. The brand is then a collection of shared experiences aimed at creating alignment between your vision and customer aspiration.

CHAPTER

# [ WHY USER EXPERIENCE IS CRITICAL TO CUSTOMER RELATIONSHIPS ]

Nothing is a waste of time if you use the experience wisely.

—Auguste Rodin

The dynamics that govern the relationship between brands and customers are evolving. But even in this era of engagement and two-way conversations, shared experiences, and connected consumerism, the reality is that the relationship businesses hope to have with customers through these new devices, applications, or networks and their true state are not one and the same.[1] In fact, it is woefully one-sided, and usually not to the advantage of customers.

Rather than examine the role new technologies and platforms can play in improving customer relationships and experiences, many businesses invest in "attendance" strategies where a brand is present in both trendy and established channels, but there's no focus on defining meaningful experiences or outcomes. Simply stated, businesses are underestimating the significance of customer experiences in even the briefest of exchanges.

Some of the biggest trends today—mobile, geo-location, social, real time—are changing how consumers discover and share information and connect with one another. Technology aside, consumers are driving the rapid adoption of technology because of the capabilities that are unlocked through each device. From self-expression and validation to communication and connections to knowledge and collaboration, new opportunities are available in each new device and platform.

As smart and connected technology matures beyond a luxury into everyday commodities, consumer expectations increase. As a result, functionality, connectedness, and experiences emerge as lures for attention. For brands to compete for attention now takes something greater than mere presences in the right channels or support for the most popular devices. Experience is much more than a moment—experience is about a movement.

For those who live in the world of design and development, user experience (UX) is sovereign. For those unfamiliar with the term, looking beyond mere website design, UX is the art and science of shaping how people feel about a product or how they engage with a service. UX is a critical enabler of meaningful and shareable experiences and, therefore, its role in the future of business and customer satisfaction is vital. An empowered UX team can provide a powerful competitive advantage.

UX is much more than design and development. Yet among executives, UX is misunderstood and often undervalued if it's acknowledged at all. But the message that I want to send to decision makers throughout the organization is that your UX team could be among the most informed and capable to improve customer experiences, relationships, loyalty, and overall business performance.

# Why?

To connected customers, experience is everything. They don't just buy products. They don't just surf sites. They don't randomly engage in social networks or everyday apps. They want experiences. It is what they buy. It is what they embrace. It is what they share.

In this social and connected economy UX is a key competitive advantage and is instrumental in how your business recognizes customers to compete for experiences now and in the future. For without thoughtful UX, consumers meander without direction, reward, or utility. And their attention, and ultimately loyalty, follows.

# THE CRUX OF ENGAGEMENT IS INTENTION AND PURPOSE

Before we can tackle product design or product experiences, we must first recognize the role customers play in our business today and articulate how we envision relationships and experiences evolving over time.

Let's start with a look at how companies approach new media today. Embracing new networks such as Facebook and Twitter, placing social and "viral" content on YouTube and in blogs, creating mobile apps and QR codes, hosting Pinteresting boards for products, is all fine and good. But, even in the design of these new media strategies, many experiences consumers are having are vague, disjointed, or undefined. There is very little vision that goes into defining relationships and experiences in each of the networks as it is, let alone creating a holistic or consistent experience across every channel.

In many ways, experiences take a back seat to engagement. Rather than looking at people and the experiences we want them to have, businesses tend to look at new technology as the crux of engagement. However, without defining the experiences that establish how people should think and feel, or what they should do next, engagement will always underperform against expectations.

Rather than looking at people and the experiences we want them to have, businesses tend to look at new technology as the crux of engagement. This is because many organizations suffer from what I call *medium-alism*, where inordinate value and weight are placed on the technology of any medium rather than on amplifying platform strengths and ideas to deliver desired and beneficial experiences and outcomes. Said another way, businesses are designing for the sake of designing, without regard for how someone feels, thinks, or acts as a result.

Rather than designing to evoke human emotion, platforms and devices take precedence over the human connection or aftereffect. Often products, pages, profiles, and entire click paths are narcissistic in their overture in that they take into account the needs of decision makers and stakeholders over that of the customers they're designed to entice. Often, the need to plug into trends trumps the opportunity to innovate and improve the customer journey.

Businesses also fall victim to what I refer to as *creative endowment.* This is a phenomenon in which creative professionals bestow upon executives their ideas for campaign. Here, technology becomes the stage for imagination without regard for the customer experience. Instead, these ideas, no matter how brilliant, are thrust on customer senses, what they see, hear, and touch, for the sake of executing against an idea rather than evoking a sensation or designing an outcome. This isn't necessarily a new phenomenon, but it is a problem.

Thankfully, there's a cure for medium-alism and creative endowment. UX is the new Rx for most new media deployments. UX goes beyond transitional user experience. From social networks to mobile apps to commerce to digital to product unboxing or usage, experiential strategies form the bridge where intentions meet outcomes. By starting with the end in mind, UX packages efficiency and enchantment to deliver more meaningful, engaging, and rewarding consumer journeys.

# It's easier said than done, however.

UX is an art and science, and it is all but ignored in the development of new media channels where customers control their own fate. If the appeal of an app diminishes, it's removed from the device. If a brand page in a social or mobile network no longer delivers value, a customer can effortlessly unlike, unfollow, or unsubscribe. If the rewards for taking action on behalf of a brand—think check-ins, QR, bar code scans, or augmented reality plays—are intangible, or gimmicky without intent, customers will simply power off. And, if a consumer cannot take action in your favor, within their channel of relevance, with ease and elegance, they will not see the value or return on investment (ROI) in being in your community.

Agencies, brand or product managers, developers, consultants, and anyone responsible for any element of customer engagement can learn from the art and science of UX. To that end, UX is a role that should, in some way, shape, or form, find a home within the design of any experiential strategy today. And, eventually, if not already, UX should take residence in any function dedicated to product development and customer experience.

**So you must ask:**

- Who owns UX?

- Is UX connected to other critical business functions?

- Who owns mobile design and experiences today?

- Who understands the engagement dynamics of Facebook, Twitter, Google+, and other new networks and the difference in behavior between these networks and your website?

- Who on your team is a master of social science to better understand engagement, behavior, and expectations?

Often, creative strategies are driven by a clever idea and not necessarily an idea supported by an engaging design or experience. At the same time, many campaigns are developed for a medium or an event where the platform takes precedence over sentiment or desired results. When considered, the formula of experiences and outcomes is incredibly potent. But when deployed without direction, everything that results is left to happenstance.

# Why risk it when you can design for it?

# THE EXPERIENCE REDUX

Certainly many brands are guilty of deploying technology strategies without designing a holistic experience. It's the reason the result of a QR scan is a web page that's—unsurprisingly—not optimized for mobile devices. It's simply unacceptable that a QR experience would lead to a web page, anyway. Or what about the enthusiasm that precedes an Augmented Reality (AR) code? Your customers might think that a digital diorama is cute, but the novelty quickly fades.

Consider for a moment the curiosity that people feel going into either one of those scenarios. There's a sense of mystery, curiosity, and anticipation for what comes next. Measuring ROI is the least of your worries here. Customer disappointment is the unintentional result of a thoughtless experience. Intent or desired outcomes are often thwarted by their very design, or lack thereof.

The primary function of UX is the development of an architecture that creates a delightful, emotional, and sensory experience. This is why it's vital to customer experiences and engagement. UX is, among many things, designed to be experiential, effective, useful, productive, and entertaining. And, most importantly, it's devised with an end in mind where the means to that end is efficient and optimized for each scenario and channel.

Let's take a look at the point of origin for the moment. Your smart phone, PC screen, and tablet open a window to a new experience that is unique to that device. It's a looking glass into your world that goes beyond usability. Successful UX evokes engagement or purpose, affects sentiment, and influences behavior. And this is why UX is so important.

As Marshall McLuhan once said, "The medium is the message." Now, the medium is not only the message, the medium is the experience. And that is why we cannot simply design for the medium; we must design the experience where the medium becomes an enabler to the journey and the end as devised.

Two words come to mind here: mission and purpose. Jesse James Garrett, author of *The Elements of User Experience*, once observed, "An information architect makes information work for people." If we use his perspective as a springboard for new media, what businesses need now are new CEOs—chief experience officers. Brands must employ experience architects, as it is they who will carry the responsibility of designing the customer journey so that it is engaging, worthy of sharing, and unified regardless of platform.

Engagement is not a product or a campaign; it's a continuum where experience is an enabler for a greater vision, mission, and outcome. And as such, the attention, impressions, and shared expressions that result are indeed reflective of what is both earned and deserved.

# USER EXPERIENCE BECOMES THE CUSTOMER EXPERIENCE:
## PRINCIPLES AND PILLARS OF UX

As in new media, when it comes to the development of customer-facing products, apps, displays, and destinations, businesses often miss two of the most critical elements for true customer engagement: evoking desired experiences and establishing desired sentiment. With the rapid innovation in technology, access becomes a commodity. Smart devices now extend, enable, and empower everyday customer behavior. And as a result, tablets, smart phones, PCs, the Internet of things, open new windows for engaging consumer touch points and defining meaningful customer journeys. How organizations are embracing this opportunity today is only part of the story.

While technology is part of the storyline, it is in fact only a chapter in a bigger story about how technology can deliver meaningful user experiences and lead to more engaging customer relationships.

# MEDIUM-ALISM EQUALS FAUX ENGAGEMENT

Now more than ever, user experience (UX) as a philosophy and as a practice serves as the architecture between customer engagement and resulting actions and sentiment. The problem is that businesses tend to have a narrow view of customer needs or expectations. More importantly, executives aren't inviting UX teams to the table around critical business, product, and customer strategy development. UX brings a unique blend of empathy and understanding, which is a powerful ingredient during any creative or innovation session.

Human emotion and behavior are rousing and among the most influential elements in experience design. I'd like to share an example with you. But before I do, I need to preface it with a disclaimer. The person I'm going to talk about, as a character, is the very antithesis of UX. But it is in this rare moment, where this character evokes personal memories and emotions for one brief moment, that he is human. He is the very person he is trying to reach.

I can't help but think back to the *Mad Men* episode where Don Draper presents his touching concept for Kodak's new wheel, aka "The Carousel": www.youtube.com/watch?v=suRDUFpsHus

In a dimly lit room and in a vulnerable voice, Draper takes us on a touching passage, "Technology is a glittering lure. But, there is the rare occasion where the public can be engaged at a level beyond flash . . . if they have a sentimental bond with the product."

Draper tells the story of his first in-house advertising job at a fur company and how his co-worker, a Greek copywriter named Teddy, explained the importance of combining what's new with emotion. "He . . . talked about a deeper bond with a product, nostalgia. It's delicate, but potent. Teddy told me that in Greek, nostalgia literally means the pain from an old wound. It's a twinge in your heart, far more powerful than memory alone."

Nostalgia, indeed, is a potent play. In this gripping scene, Draper doesn't push a creative idea for the sake of the idea; instead he takes technology and makes it human. He makes it so human, in fact, that as you watch the scene, it becomes intimate, and it becomes personal. As such, viewers are reminded of the memories that they miss or cherish and for that moment, their experiences join the confluence of emotion, brand, and technology.

Here's the important part . . . that scene—let's pretend that was really the campaign Kodak considered—was designed to do just as I described. And, that's the point. That campaign as conveyed would take center stage where technology, media, design, and the overall experience would be designed to evoke emotions and trigger a desired effect in any network or any platform or device.

This is the beginning of an important shift where neither technology nor creativity will lead the strategy for developing and steering customer experiences. Instead, intention and aspiration become the North Star. Technology and creativity merely become the enablers in the delivery of magical experiences and gratifying sentiment.

# THE JUXTAPOSITION OF EMPATHY AND EXPERIENCE

In UX, user experiences are interwoven with absorbing visual design packaged in a journey rich with empathy and desire. For UX to be effective, customer experience and design architects must first feel it. Effective engagement is inspired by *empathy* that develops simply by *being human.* It takes a holistic approach to truly deliver an empathetic voyage. Design, channels, and devices are not enough. It takes a culture of customer-centricity to feel their challenges and ambitions and what it is that they need or do not know they need. Again, it takes a vision and a higher purpose to inspire beneficial outcomes.

Businesses must reimagine the future of customer relationships and not only vocalize it, but express it as a working charter. It requires nothing short of a culture shift to truly appreciate the customers for not only what they can do but also how they feel.

Like so many things related to technology and new media, champions tend to push a bottom-up strategy. But, what must take place must complement the current groundswell by convincing executives and decision makers to lead top-down strategies that convey a vision for what customer experiences should involve. Only then can we inspire incredible UX to in turn bring that experience to life. Everything starts with defining a vision that articulates the view of the customer journey not just as you see it, but what it is that customers would appreciate, relate to, and value.

Vision is device- and platform-agnostic. But as Mr. Draper expresses in *Mad Men*, it's indeed "delicate, but potent."

Businesses that place people and what they feel, think, do, and share as a priority in not just product design but overall marketing and business strategy outperform those who don't. It's about a journey that knows no end—only how to keep the passengers delighted and valued.

CHAPTER

15

[ INNOVATE OR DIE ]

Good judgment comes from experience, and experience comes from bad judgment.

—Barry LePatner

By now you see that earning relevance requires much more than the adoption of the latest technologies or launching endeavors in the latest social or app flavor of the month.

In the last few chapters we learned the importance of user experience in product design and our overall channel strategies. It is through technology channels, though, that we reach customers in the moments of truth to favorably guide their journey. These channels aren't selected arbitrarily. They are specifically chosen to serve a purpose, to meet a need, and to elicit a desired outcome.

With all of the technology options and opportunities facing your organization, where do you even start? Believe it or not, it is in this very moment where your strategy will earn its merit. Without matching technology investments with customer behavior in the moments of truth and aligning everything with business outcomes, your strategy will earn the failure it deserves. We're in this together, so let's work together in this chapter to prioritize opportunities and place wise investments where they'll count. In the process, we'll develop a culture for recognizing emerging technology to adopt the right platforms before they become disruptive.

What is Disruptive Technology? Let's take a moment to define it. Disruptive technology is the ongoing innovations that emerge without expectation to introduce a new capability or solution that creates a market and value network at the expense of an existing market and value network.[1] This is important because many organizations are investing in emerging technology for customer engagement, metrics, marketing and advertising, internal collaboration and education, HR, product development, and so on. But they do so without the clearest picture into overall direction, long-term strategy, or even a deep understanding of the expectations and obstacles that exist among customers and employees.

If we look at how organizations experiment with popular mobile and social platforms such as Facebook, Twitter, Instagram, Foursquare, Google+, Klout, Pinterest, and a whole list of others, we're left to wonder whether a divide and conquer strategy really isn't just another guise where businesses become a jack-of-all trades but a master of none.

## That's not the strategy we're going to pursue together . . .

# CMOs ARE AT THE CROSSROADS OF CUSTOMER TRANSACTIONS AND ENGAGEMENT

At the intersection of relevance and obsolescence is the ability to recognize opportunities for change based on shifting consumer behavior and the subtle coalescence between emerging and disruptive technology.[2] Your businesses must learn that change is taking place today with or without you. To what extent varies from company to company. But without an understanding of how technology and society are evolving and how decisions are influenced and made, businesses are left to make decisions in the dark.

We all know how difficult, if not nearly impossible, it is to change. We also realize that once we do begin the inevitable process of transformation, the distance between where we are and where we need to be is not expeditious in any sense. In the era of Digital Darwinism, the journey toward evolution and revolution is, in fact, the destination. It is perpetual.[3]

This is a time I must implore you to think differently. New technology, platforms, and channels are not the catalysts for change, but merely among its agents. For example, while Facebook and Twitter are often the recipients of accolades for their roles in fueling revolutions, we must remember that they are the networks that facilitate engagement.

In the world of business, customers are using new technology to share experiences. And, those experiences are either to your benefit or detriment. As Mark Cuban, owner of the Dallas Mavericks and chairman of HDNet, shared in *The End of Business as Usual*, "To be successful in business, you need to see what others don't." To that I would also add, "and do what others won't or can't."[4]

# THROUGH A TELESCOPE, WE BRING THE WORLD CLOSER—THROUGH A MICROSCOPE, WE SEE WHAT WAS PREVIOUSLY INVISIBLE TO THE NAKED EYE

I often say, "in brevity, there's clarity." Although I still believe this to be true, I also see that there's a delicate balance necessary in understanding what is hype and what is truly disruptive. Therefore, we must look forward and at the same time, look closer at what's taking place right now to analyze true impact. Separating fact from fiction or hype from disruption is now part of our job as our consumers are driving these results based on what they adopt, how they communicate, and how they influence and are influenced in decision-making cycles. With so much information and change before us, where do we focus?

To help, IBM reached out to more than 1,700 chief marketing officers (CMOs), spanning 19 industries and 64 countries as part of its CMO study, one of the C-suite studies conducted by IBM's Institute for Business Value.[5] The goal was to learn how consumer behavior and technology are changing business focus, forecasts, and decisions. The results are both illuminating and helpful.

## So, what's keeping everyone up at night?

As you can see, big data, social media, and the myriad of available consumer channels and devices make up the top three trends leading to corporate insomnia. But beyond those trends, the entire list is fascinating and worthy of study.

## Percent of CMOs reporting underpreparedness

50%

| | |
|---|---|
| Data explosion | 71% |
| Social media | 68% |
| Growth of channel and device choices | 65% |
| Shifting consumer demographics | 63% |
| Financial constraints | 59% |
| Decreasing brand loyalty | 57% |
| Growth market opportunities | 56% |
| ROI accountability | 56% |
| Customer collaboration and influence | 56% |
| Privacy considerations | 55% |
| Global outsourcing | 54% |
| Regulatory considerations | 50% |
| Corporate transparency | 47% |

## Expected level of complexity and preparedness to handle

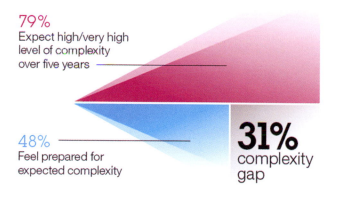

**79%**
Expect high/very high
level of complexity
over five years

**48%**
Feel prepared for
expected complexity

**31%**
complexity
gap

If we break out the expected level of complexity and preparedness to handle what lies ahead in terms of emerging versus disruptive technology, we surface what IBM refers to as the complexity gap.

The IBM CMO study also reinforces my research and experiences with leading enterprises.[6] Businesses do indeed seek to get closer to customers.

**To that end, CMOs believe that there are three key areas for improvement:**

**1** Deliver value to empowered customers.

**2** Foster lasting connections.

**3** Capture value and measure results.

Addressing each of these items unlocks the true essence of the trends that are disrupting businesses today . . . customers are becoming increasingly connected and as a result, they are empowered, influential, and increasingly elusive.

As Ann Glover, chief marketing officer, ING Insurance U.S., shared in the research report, "Customers today have more control and influence with the brand than ever. We need to make sure it's give and take—a two-sided conversation, with both parties having responsibilities in the interaction."

Market research has helped to guide executive decisions over the years. Nowadays, however, market research is simply studying the equivalent of a mass audience without surfacing the nuances that define the audience with an audience of audiences.[7] The study found that 75 percent of CMOs use customer analytics to mine data, but only 42 percent study customer reviews and only 26 percent track blogs. What CMOs are largely missing is context and the ability to foster empathetic strategies and supporting protocol.

As we can clearly see, CMOs are missing the ability to extract and introduce a truly human touch, focusing on markets rather than individuals.[8]

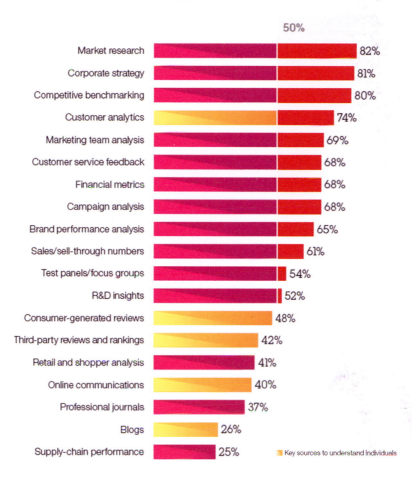

**Sources used to influence strategy decisions**

| Source | Percentage |
|---|---|
| Market research | 82% |
| Corporate strategy | 81% |
| Competitive benchmarking | 80% |
| Customer analytics | 74% |
| Marketing team analysis | 69% |
| Customer service feedback | 68% |
| Financial metrics | 68% |
| Campaign analysis | 68% |
| Brand performance analysis | 65% |
| Sales/sell-through numbers | 61% |
| Test panels/focus groups | 54% |
| R&D insights | 52% |
| Consumer-generated reviews | 48% |
| Third-party reviews and rankings | 42% |
| Retail and shopper analysis | 41% |
| Online communications | 40% |
| Professional journals | 37% |
| Blogs | 26% |
| Supply-chain performance | 25% |

Key sources to understand individuals

If you take a look at the graph above, it's these traditional metrics that drive increasingly ineffective decisions at a time when those very decisions are starting to also work against the company.[9] Customer analytics is at least in the fourth spot, but as you can see, it isn't until we get down to the 50 percent mark that personal data factors into strategic decisions. And even today, blogs are just a mere 26 percent.

# CUSTOMER ENGAGEMENT IS NOT THE SAME AS CONVERSATIONS

Remember, at the top of the list of priorities of CEOs is getting closer to customers. Yet, looking at this information, it's clear that the customer and the idea of the true picture of customers are contrasting. To truly engage, businesses must not only understand customers, but also act. It really is a play on the old saying, "actions speak louder than words." But here, actions speak as loudly as words and, therefore, anything social requires social action.

When I was writing *The End of Business as Usual,* I sought out a working definition of the word *engagement*. It was both unbelievable and also understandable that the results were varied and confusing. I proposed a working definition in the manuscript that explained engagement as the act of a consumer and an organization or brand interacting within the consumer's network of relevance. Engagement, and here's the important part, is then measured by the takeaway value, sentiment, and resulting actions following the interaction. This is the experience.

**Extensive use of customer data**

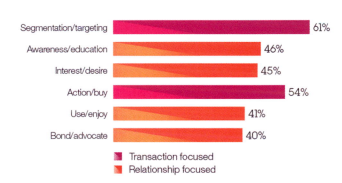

With this definition in mind, we zero in on the discrepancy between how businesses view the customer and how they measure *engagement*.

According to the IBM CMO study, CMOs (Chief Marketing Officers) reveal that data is focused on managing the customer transaction and not the relationship. This is not engagement. And, this is why I believe that any discussion about sCRM (social customer relationship management) is premature at best. As the following data demonstrates, companies are still placing greater emphasis on the "M" and not the "R" or relationship.

Yes, this is the end of business as usual and rather than merely focus on the transaction, businesses must focus on creating a meaningful and shareable customer experience first. In the preceding chart, we can see that awareness/education, interest/desire, use/enjoy, and bond/advocate make the list. And, the direct beneficiary of those initiatives is the customer.

Engagement is not just about communication. It's about creating experiences that mean something, something that's positive and worth sharing. And, that is what's possible today. In fact, if we look beyond transactions and measure results as they define and drive experiences, we can expand our toolbox to include what I refer to as the *A.R.T. of Engagement*. How can we best use our customers' networks or services of relevance to inspire or spark actions, reactions, and transactions? How can we shape experiences and outcomes?

Nick Barton, vice president of sales and marketing, Greater China, InterContinental Hotel Group shared his brief but potent thoughts on the subject in IBM's report. "We have to get scientific about the customer experience."

**Seven most important measures to gauge marketing success**

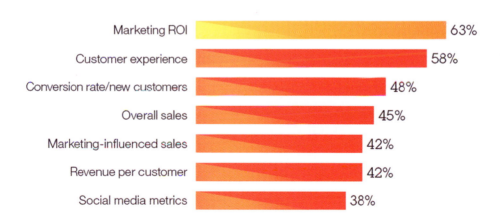

IBM found that at the top of the list is the now infamous quest for what seems like seeking the holy grail without a map, return on investment (ROI).[10] But there's hope, as customer experience is second on the list. Truly, with the customer experience defined from beginning to end, the other metrics fall into place.

Actions speak as loudly as words and as CMOs focus their priorities for shifts toward disruptive technology, the customer is at the front and center of corporate transformation.

**Priorities for managing the shift toward digital technologies**

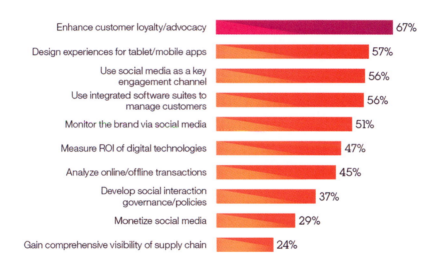

Everything comes down to customer relationships and experiences and that's what will separate your strategies from tomorrow's success stories. To that end, at the top of the list is enhancing customer loyalty and advocacy. Following is designing experiences for tablets and mobile devices. Third, CMOs will use social media as a key engagement (hopefully as defined earlier) channel. Now we're talking! As you can see below, those companies that focus on customer-focused *and* business outcomes perform well.

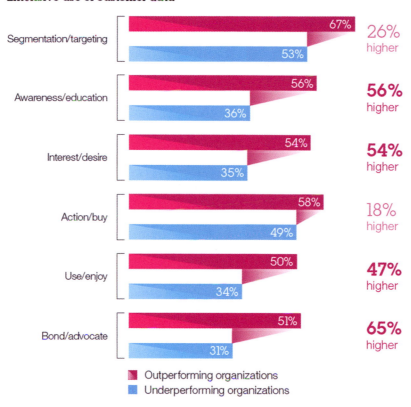

**Extensive use of customer data**

| | Outperforming organizations | Underperforming organizations | |
|---|---|---|---|
| Segmentation/targeting | 67% | 53% | 26% higher |
| Awareness/education | 56% | 36% | 56% higher |
| Interest/desire | 54% | 35% | 54% higher |
| Action/buy | 58% | 49% | 18% higher |
| Use/enjoy | 50% | 34% | 47% higher |
| Bond/advocate | 51% | 31% | 65% higher |

■ Outperforming organizations
■ Underperforming organizations

IBM found that CMOs who use customer data to improve customer experiences are actually outperforming those businesses that do not invest additional effort in fostering customer relationships. This is the chart that should bring it home for you. This *is* what you're fighting for. This is data to savor as it demonstrates the end of business as usual and the beginning of a new era of relevance. You are the change agent and your organization, your team, your peers, need you now more than ever.

# TEN PRIORITIES FOR MEANINGFUL BUSINESS TRANSFORMATION

Surviving Digital Darwinism is only part of the story. From the IBM CMO study, we learned that it takes customer-centricity and the ability to prioritize investments. But, more importantly, it takes leadership and it takes courage to do and see what others won't or can't. The future of business and customer and employee engagement is built on a foundation of vision, trust, significance, and relationships. Set on this foundation are 10 pillars on which your business transformation is predicated.

**Leadership:** As technology continues to evolve & permeate work & life, behavior, expectations & communication evolve. Someone must look ahead, see where we need to go & lead the way to relevance.

**Vision:** The stated outlook of organizational direction needs review. In a time when brands are co-created, if vision is unclear or underwhelming, alignment, community & camaraderie are elusive.

**Strategy:** With new media & technology creating a groundswell of customer empowerment, new strategies must focus on alignment, objectives & meaningful experiences & outcomes.

**Philanthropic Capitalism:** Customers expect values to match their own. A new era of CSR requires charitable & sustainable decisions as part of everyday business where customers become stakeholders.

**Culture:** This is a time of change, which requires coalescence & solidarity. Organizations need to focus on cultivating a culture of adaptation, customer & employee centricity & empowerment.

**Intelligence:** Social media is introducing the art & science of listening & monitoring to marketing/service teams. Organizations need to invest in technology, teams & processes to learn & feed insights.

**People:** The 5th P of the marketing mix, People, will take center stage as organizations empower employees to experiment through intrapreneurialsim & partner with customers to advance products, services & processes.

**Localization:** For global organizations hoping to connect with customers around the world, localization & contextualization are king in any engagement strategy.

**Influence:** Digital influence is becoming prominent, turning everyday consumers into new influentials. Organizations should ID & engage to extend reach. Contributing to networks will also earn influence.

**Innovation:** Adapt or Die! The ability to recognize new opportunities, disruptive technology & the capacity to consider or develop new solutions, responses & systems as a matter of process & collaboration.

TRENDS FOR TRANSFORMATION

BRIAN SOLIS

These 10 principles serve as the framework for an adaptable business model where opportunities are readily assessed and innovation is regularly practiced. The reward is relevance, affinity, and advocacy. As Leon C. Megginson once said in paraphrasing Charles Darwin's *Origin of the Species*,

> " It is not the strongest of the species that survives, nor the most intelligent that survives. It is the one that is most adaptable to change. "

**Vision:** The stated outlook of organizational direction needs review. When's the last time you read your company's vision or mission statement? If you have read it recently, would you tweet it proudly? In a time when brands are not created, but instead co-created, if vision is unclear or underwhelming, alignment, community, and camaraderie will prove elusive.

**Strategy:** With new media and emerging technology creating a groundswell of customer empowerment, new strategies must focus on the alignment of objectives with meaningful experiences and outcomes. All too often, emerging technology is confused with disruptive technology, where it impacts how companies work or how customers behave. Far too much emphasis, budget, and time are placed in new media channels without an understanding of why or what it is that customers expect or appreciate.

**Culture:** This is a time of change, which requires coalescence and solidarity. We can't change whether the culture is rigid or risk averse. We can't innovate if those who experiment are not supported. Organizations need to focus on cultivating a culture of adaptation rooted in customer- and employee-centricity and, more importantly, empowerment. Culture is everything. It is and should be intentional. It should be designed. Those companies that invest in the development of an adaptive culture will realize improved relationships that contribute to competitive advantages.

**People:** The fifth *P* of the marketing mix, "People," will take center stage. Organizations that embrace the spirit of intrepreneurialism will empower employees to experiment through failure and success to improve engagement and morale. And, by embracing customers, insights will inspire relevant products, services, and processes. I'll also add one more that aligns vision with people. The sixth *P* of marketing is "Purpose." Aspiring to a higher purpose is what separates mediocrity from performance and relevance. And, purpose is a pillar of experience.

**Innovation:** The ability to recognize new opportunities is perhaps the greatest challenge rivaled only by the ability to execute. Emerging and disruptive technology is now part of the business landscape and customer lifestyle. Innovation, trends, and hype are not going to stop. In fact, they will only amplify. The capacity to identify and consider new solutions and responses is critical. It must be supported by innovative collaboration and decision-making processes and systems to assess and react. Innovation must be perpetual.

**Influence:** Digital influence is becoming prominent in social networks, turning everyday consumers into new influentials. As a result, a new customer hierarchy is developing that forces businesses to identify and engage those who rank higher than others. There is no future in any business model that is cemented in reactive engagement. Organizations should identify and engage all connected customers to extend reach outside of problems. Businesses must engage when touch points emerge, during decision-making cycles, when positive experiences are shared, or to proactively feed the results of those who are searching for insight and direction. Contributing value to people and investing time and energy into networks of relevance will earn any organization a position of equal or greater influence.

**Localization:** For global organizations hoping to connect with customers around the world, localization and contextualization are king in any engagement strategy. This is also true for any engagement strategy regardless of locale. Many companies are jumping on every bandwagon imaginable, syndicating content, thinning resources, and investing no more in each network than what's necessary to maintain a pulse. Facebook, Twitter, Google+, YouTube, Foursquare, Instagram, Pinterest, and Quora become broadcast channels for one-to-many strategies and programs that do very little for cultivating dedicated and engaged communities.

**Intelligence:** One of the biggest trends in 2011 was the development of social media command centers. At the heart of these sophisticated data-gathering silos were conversations and tools that allowed community managers to listen, respond, and promote engagement within the company. While social media is introducing the art and science of monitoring to marketing and service teams, it is the organizations that invest in technology, teams, and processes that will translate activity into actionable insights.

**Philanthropic Capitalism:** Customers expect values to match their own core values. What used to be a necessary checklist of community focus, such as corporate social responsibility or CSR, is now rebooted. Philanthropic capitalism is a business model where companies contribute to worthwhile causes on behalf of customers as part of the transaction. Additionally, customers are expressing that they will also invest in companies where employees are "treated well," pledging trust and loyalty as a result. The empathetic business model on the horizon requires charitable and sustainable decisions as part of everyday business where customers naturally become stakeholders.

# DISRUPTIVE TECHNOLOGY AND HOW TO COMPETE FOR THE FUTURE

Although disruptive technology is the bearer of tremendous opportunity, it is equally a harbinger of obsolescence. Technology's impact on society and business is substantial. As technology continues to become part of everyday life, it becomes a continuous disruptive cycle that forever evolves how people communicate, work, and connect.

Keeping up requires a perpetual investment as innovation is constant and it's only increasing. We are becoming a culture rife with ingenuity. Entrepreneurialism is contagious. The start-up way, or the "hacker life" as lived and breathed by Facebook, is introducing new mind-sets and models and it's inspiring all who taste it to code, design, build, invest, and take risks.[11] And this is just the beginning. Innovation is a global movement and it's gaining momentum.

This is a time to take a step back, recognize where we are and where we need to be, examine our strategies and current initiatives, review our investments and opportunities, and consider new areas for change or new pursuits.

The truth is that innovation works for us and against us. Investing in it with purpose and design is our responsibility. Whether you're an entrepreneur leading the latest or the next hot start-up, a business executive seeking solutions or a competitive edge, a decision maker or a champion for change in any industry, this is the time to see through the chaos of features, trends, IPOs, investments, ballooning valuations, and so on, to clear a path for meaningful progress.

Part of the challenge is knowing when to recognize opportunities. Although it's easy to get caught up in the hype, there is a gap that exists between current needs, evolving pains, and the myriad of solutions hitting desktops, smart phones, tablets, and digital appliances every day. The problem is that many organizations aren't designed to be adaptive. They're designed to optimize efficiencies and processes. But, times have changed and disruptive technology isn't as easy to recognize nor capitalize on without a greater mission and purpose or an infrastructure to identify trends, experiment, learn, and scale.

Competing for the future requires a full assessment of how some of the biggest trends in technology impact your business or markets today and how they will influence behavior in the future. While this list may alter, expand, or contract based on your industry, the image below should provide a glimpse of just how expansive the landscape is, and while not every technology is affecting the bottom line today, elements are beginning to change the way decisions are made and how people work with one another. At the very least, the golden triangle of cloud, mobile, and social provides a hub to begin the evaluation of both technology and human behavior.

## WHEEL OF DISRUPTION

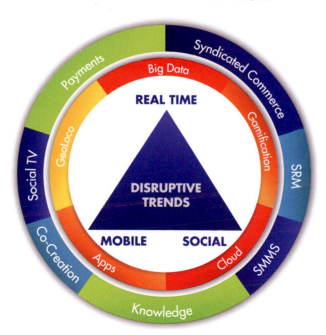

**To chart a new course toward relevance, here are five initial steps to consider:**

**1** Assume that there is a surplus of confusion among users and decision makers within organizations and customers on which technology is trending versus technology that is showing signs of becoming or already is disruptive. Discovering the difference and prioritizing what's important is critical.

**2** Understand that the roles of the CMO and CIO (Chief Information Officer) are becoming closer than ever before. With marketing investing a significant percentage of the overall technology budget now and over time, the "I" in CIO may need to represent innovation to help lead more informed decisions from the inside.

**3** Task an existing organization, external partner, or develop a new task force to evaluate technology to improve the infrastructure of how your business works; cultivate relationships with customers, employees, and stakeholders; design better products and services, and demonstrate competitive advantages.

**4** Deploy this team to measure technology against a myriad of factors that are important to your business and assess which technologies are worthy of implementation, financial investment, acquisition, or experimentation.

**5** Realign the team against a renewed vision and purpose and train employees to use these technologies to achieve desired objectives at the enterprise, LoB (line of business), and functional levels . . . to meet customer and employee expectations and steer delightful experiences.[12]

These are the times when getting caught up in technology, value, and new technology is often mistaken for innovation that inflates the dreaded bubble. What we don't need is to invest in the wrong technologies simply because posts are constantly written with the "top 10" ways to grow our business with said platform. While we can watch them grow, the real focus should be on the development of a formal system that measures impact and prioritizes resources around it accordingly.

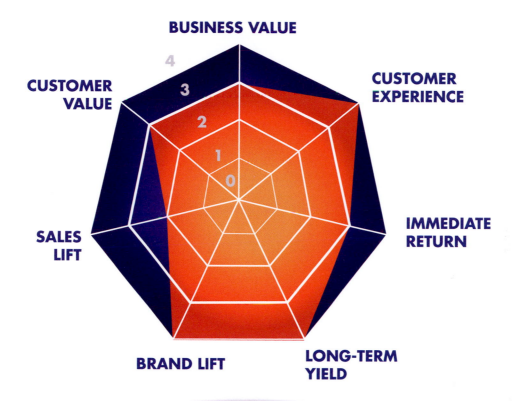

Measuring technology's impact on business, opportunities, and customer experiences

Building a process for disruptive technology sets the stage for a culture of innovation and adaptation. Customers aren't the only passengers on the dynamic journey. As the change agent for your organization, as the hero, you will lead your organization on its own journey of transformation. And in doing so, you will help your business earn relevance now and in the future where success is measured in revenue, profitability, relationships, and shared experiences.

CHAPTER

16

# THE DILEMMA'S INNOVATOR

Art begins in imitation and ends in innovation.

—Mason Cooley

In a time when only one in five U.S. adults does not use the Internet, it takes an astute command of the obvious to see that society is becoming increasingly digital and connected.[1] As a result of this profound connectedness, a gap is already forming between people and your business. A gap is also manifesting between consumer expectations and the products and services you offer.

The simple truth is that it takes a culture of innovation to compete for both Generation C and for the future . . . and that's where you come in. You are the hero in this journey, and the change you lead starting with evolving customer engagement and defining experiences will have a great effect within your business. One of the greatest opportunities before you is materialized through the evolution in connected consumerism. How your organization is designed and structured today will one day work against you if organization transformation is on your agenda. As you more than well know, management, processes, systems, and rewards are constructed to improve what "is" today and not what "will be" or "should be." To innovate first requires innovation within.

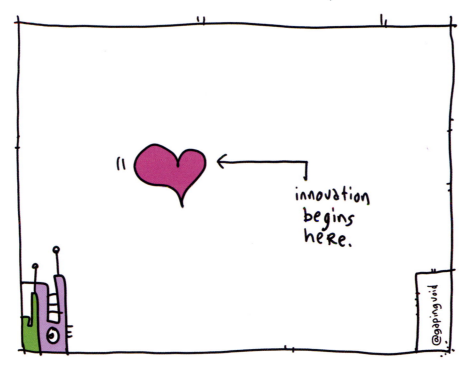

# INNOVATION IS BLINDNESS: WHY INNOVATION IS FUNDAMENTAL TO THE SURVIVAL OF TOMORROW'S BUSINESS . . . TODAY

In the book *The Innovator's Dilemma*, Clayton Christensen introduced the term *Disruptive Innovation* to demonstrate how and why successful businesses failed. Christensen looked at many companies including Sears, DEC, and Xerox. These companies were once celebrated for business, management, and market leadership, only to become symbols of corporate laggards and examples of what could happen without transformation. While his initial hypothesis was that each of the companies had in one way or another stopped competing and innovating, he in fact learned the opposite. The culture and supporting structure of each company shared commonsensical and seemingly smart tenets:

- Each company possessed great management teams.
- They listened to customers.
- Improved products and services.
- Invested in R&D while focusing on profits.
- Pioneered innovation.
- Sought to grow revenues and market share.

Yet these companies lost their once prestigious edge simply because they did the right things over and over. While they focused on running what they knew, they missed what they didn't know. Sounds paradoxical, I know. The trends that literally disrupted and continue to disrupt markets result from shifts in behavior, expectations, new business models, and left-field products and services that either contributed to or serendipitously aligned with these shifts.

Businesses that thrust the Sears, DECs, and Xeroxes of the world into complacency or borderline irrelevance, championed Christensen's Disruptive Innovation simply by doing business. Either intentionally or unknowingly, emerging competitors pursued unusual or even counterintuitive business practices that garnered incredible traction.

First, Christensen found that products that possessed qualities for Disruptive Innovation weren't good enough for existing customers. Established companies listened to customers and to appease them, delivered more of what they wanted.

Once a product becomes mainstream, it is at risk of becoming a commodity. Once commoditized, profits dwindle and as a result, supporting processes automate and optimize to preserve margins.

For years, people asked for cheaper, smaller laptops and that's just what they got. Unfortunately, they also got what they paid for. In the meantime, Apple introduced stylish, more expensive, intuitive, and often heavier/larger laptops to those who never knew they needed a new computing experience.

Second, Christensen learned that there is no profitable market for products that carry the Disruptive Innovation banner. Markets for the "next big thing" would already be the "current big thing." Companies that focus on research and development tend to look at innovation through a lens of sustained progress and not necessarily the introduction of new products, processes, or revolutions in direction or the way people work.

Apple's iPhone and iPad lines continue to prove that there is indeed a market for the next big thing. In Q4 2011, Apple sold more iPads than any other PC manufacturer sold PC devices. As the company focuses on improving existing product lines, it continues to look at its next opportunity for disruption. Many believe Apple's future product will completely disrupt the television industry.

Third, Disruptive Innovation represents a shift in value. The aim for potentially disruptive products or services will not make money through conventional means. Instead, new business models will emerge to support new solutions. For example, hard drive manufacturers pursue sustained innovation in making drives that are smaller, faster, and hold greater volumes of data. In the case of the laptop and portable market, for example, innovation in hard drives shifted from moving parts to solid state to make room for smaller footprint devices. In the case of

Google's Chromebook, for example, its onboard storage is minimal. Instead, all storage for apps and data is stored in the cloud and thus the need for laptop drives is now minimal while still delivering a productive experience for its users. The new opportunity for drive manufacturers is providing the capacity to support the cloud.

# In the circle of life, connected consumerism is the new reality. Those businesses that don't disrupt their own markets will find their markets disrupted for them.

Not all is lost, however. While Generation C is taking shape, you must look at how to innovate within to innovate outside. If Gen C'ers are your customers, they are also your employees. Now's the time to form a special unit to start exploring needs, opportunities, expectations, and behavior to develop an action plan that doesn't distract your focus, but instead invests in the alternative realities that are already taking shape.

In the end, complacency is a symptom of mediocrity and mediocrity is the result of a leadership organization that chooses not to lead, but instead, to manage how to be better or more efficient around "what is" and not "what should be" or "what's next."

# IN THE BATTLE AGAINST RELEVANCE VERSUS IRRELEVANCE: IT'S SURVIVAL OF THE FITTING

The good news is that you're not in this alone. Businesses are transforming and their examples can help you make the case within your organization. I'd like to share one example with you here. You've probably heard of Burberry. Established in 1856, this iconic fashion brand has effectively competed for relevance for more than 150 years. To do so takes constant innovation without losing your soul to compete for an evolving customer landscape that is undergoing the connected transformation we've spent so much time on throughout the book.

There are so many examples of companies that are transforming from the inside out. I chose Burberry because its complete transformation was and is inspired by the connected consumer. The company didn't just try to design its way into the lives of Generation C; instead it saw the dynamic customer journey and each moment of truth as a revelation that the company could do better.

Certainly product design and overall experience design is part of what Harry Gold of Overrdrive Interactive calls the *Brand Embrace*.[2] The term describes the sum total of all digital relationships that organizations can create with their prospects and customers. When I think about the idea of the Brand Embrace in the context of connected consumerism and the new era of experiences that they expect, I envision the Brand Embrace as the articulation of a vision for the desired relationship between brand and customer. This vision also conveys the experience a customer will have with the brand during each moment of truth. That to me is a true Brand Embrace.

Angela Ahrendts, Burberry[3] CEO, captured this vision for the Brand Embrace so eloquently: "You have to be totally connected with everyone who touches your brand."

When I look at Burberry's current endeavor, it is a series of innovations that involve not only product and customer experiences but also the behind-the-scenes investments in technology, processes, and policies. While it doesn't sound as exciting as a fashion show in London or Paris, it is the type of investment that will keep the company on the runway for years to come.

If you think about it, this is as much about new consumerism and disruptive technology as it is about culture . . . fostering an internal culture that's customer-centric, adaptive, and above all else, ready to tackle transformation.

Burberry, like so many other brands that "get it," jumped into social and mobile media. As of September 2012, the iconic fashion brand boasted 14 million Likes on Facebook. But as this book set out to demonstrate, it will take more than a Facebook brand page or brand app to engage the connected customer and set forth incredible and shareable experiences. It takes transformation in philosophy, evolution in vision, and investment in infrastructure. In working with Salesforce, that's just what Angela Ahrendts and creative director Christopher Bailey set out to accomplish.

It started with Burberry's vision to not only stay relevant, but earn a significant brand embrace, one that would create a new world for the global fashion house.

Defining the brand embrace is a critical step for defining the experience. In a promotional video published by Salesforce, Ahrendts shared the importance of vision and transformation to bring the brand embrace to life. "We had a vision, to be the first company that was fully digital end-to-end. The experience would be that a customer has total access to Burberry, across any device, anywhere. They get exactly the same feeling of the brand and feeling of the culture, regardless of how, when and where they were accessing the brand. Everyone can come to Burberry World and understand the journey and mission that Burberry is on."

It might seem like a risk for a luxury brand, one that some might say portrays a sense of exclusivity, but through an integrated approach guided by a united vision of innovation, evolution, tradition, and experience. In an article published in *Fortune* in June 2012,[4] Maureen Mullen of tech think tank L2 observed, "What they've done, that no other organization in the fashion industry has done, is put a relentless focus on digital innovation."

To bring a holistic experience to life, it would take the integration of the company, its employees, its customers, and the all-important brand. Salesforce CEO Marc Benioff met with Ahrendts and Burberry CTO John Douglas in a New York hotel. Benioff sketched out "Burberry World" to visualize how integration will enable Ahrendts' vision for an integrated customer experience across channels, devices, retail locations, and products and services. In an interview with Benioff at Cloudforce New York in 2011, Ahrendts answered an important question, "Why Burberry World?" Her answer was direct. While the company maintains important relationships with key constituencies and stakeholders across the board, 70 percent of the company's workforce is under 30. And equally, many of its new customers and prospects also represent younger demographics. These digital natives communicate and connect different, and Ahrendts recognized this in her response to Why Burberry World: "This is typically where consumers would go."

Burberry Heritage + Connected Customer + Vision for Brand Embrace + Culture + Technology = Burberry World.

What started as a crude but compelling drawing on a napkin ultimately became the blueprint for Burberry World, the company's ambitious 18-month plan to unite technology, people, retail, products, and the overarching brand. If you look closely, you can see an integrated strategy that defines and reinforces Burberry's vision to deliver a holistic experience and a desired Brand Embrace.

In the CloudForce interview, Ahrendts positioned Burberry World as the front door where connected customers can move freely across screens and instores for a holistic and personalized experience. "Every screen has the ability to move and to interact exactly as you would anything in a store that would have human interaction." Ahrendts continued, "It's mobile first. It's social first. It's e-com first . . . I think it's just flipping the traditional business model totally upside down. It's not about bricks and mortar. It's a difference universe. There's a different universal language being spoken. I think companies have to speak that language. You can't fight it. Your workforce, they speak that language, so the onus is on us to be a part of the social revolution."

The foundation for Burberry World supports several pillars that reinforce Burberry's plan to adapt the business from the inside out, traversing the back office, customer engagement, retail, each moment of truth, and building an infrastructure to lead customers through an enriching dynamic customer journey.

**It started with a sketch.**
*Source: ©2013 salesforce.com, inc. All rights reserved. Image reproduced with permission.*

Beauty without intelligence is a masterpiece painted on a napkin.

*—Unknown*

**Together with Burberry, Salesforce envisioned the 12 Pillars of a Social Enterprise:**

1. Social Customer Profile

2. Social and Digital Integration with Supply Chain Partners

**3.** Burberry Body

**4.** Mobile Apps: Runway to Reality

**5.** Listen, Analyze, Engage

**6.** Retail Stores

**7.** Social Networks (Think MOTs and DCJ)

**8.** Burberry.com

**9.** Back Office Integration

**10.** Customer Service: The Burberry Experience

**11.** Social Personalization, for a true VIP experience

**12.** Burberry World: 7,500 employees (Enterprise Social Network)

The key is to find your pillars as they will support your vision for the brand embrace and the experience you wish to envelop your customers. Not every company has a leader such as Angela Ahrendts. You'll need to lead the change, but you will require executive sponsorship. To do so, you'll need to assemble an internal steering committee that's representative of key functions throughout the organization to create a blueprint for transformation. The goal is to match your vision, the desired experience and brand embrace, the brand promise and pillars, and the corresponding technologies and philosophies it will take to enliven everything. If you are an executive, then change is well within your responsibility. This is your opportunity to lead, not just manage growth.

In closing, Ahrendts offered priceless advice with undertones of forewarning to any executive seeking to compete for relevance and compete for the future. "To any CEO who's skeptical at all, you have . . . you have to create a social enterprise today. You have to be totally connected with everyone who touches your brand. If you don't do that, I don't know what your business model is in five years."

Think digital.

CHAPTER

17

**THE HERO'S JOURNEY**

# THE HERO'S JOURNEY

Nobody can go back and start a new beginning, but anyone can start today and make a new ending.

—Maria Robinson

This book is dedicated to disruption, innovation, and transformation. As the real hero in this journey, this book is dedicated to you. My intention is to introduce you to your connected customers, demonstrate how they progress through a dynamic customer journey, and how they behave in each moment of truth. Part entitlement, part egotism, part DIY (do it yourself), and part entrepreneurialism, Generation C'ers' behavior is indeed dissimilar to that of their more traditional counterparts.

Together we've learned that these consumers are far more informed, far more sophisticated in their decision making, and savvier in their digital prowess. They're artistic and awe-inspiring in their capacity to effectively multitask across multiple devices and platforms. We have to adapt accordingly.

Now more than ever, though, leadership takes innovation and a vision for not only introducing something new, but also for something meaningful and experiential. To truly innovate, though, starts with something far simpler than transformation. Innovation starts with going back to basics to align vision and intentions with desirable outcomes and significant experiences—even if that means investing in the development of products and services that your customers don't realize they want or need yet.

**Let's recap the last 16 (yes, we're counting zero) chapters for a moment:**

**1** Connected customers open up new touch points.

**2** How your connected customers influence and are influenced is nothing like how your traditional customers are.

**3** Their expectations are different and they align with you for different reasons than you think. Quality, how you treat employees and customers, and the sustainable footprint you leave on this planet are of uppermost importance to engagement.

**4** The channels they use may not ever cross other channels. They can be fully contained from beginning to end on one device in one network.

**5** Sometimes customers do hop channels and they expect a seamless and integrated experience. You need to bring these various groups together to design a seamless experience.

**6** The one thing that your connected customers value above all is feeling valued. We need a new way to express value and measure it.

**7** To connect with connected customers takes (a) an understanding of their behavior and preferences; (b) the ability to read between the lines and innovate in products and services; (c) the definition of a vision for what customer experiences will look like in every moment of truth and throughout the dynamic customer journey; and (d) a blueprint for transforming the inside of the organization through philosophy and technology to lead a new era of integrated customer experiences and engagement.

# To change takes two things: the aspiration and determination to change.

# It starts with vision.

Chances are that your organization is already exploring new media, technology, and alternative channels for customer engagement. To start with vision is a seemingly trivial step, but its role sets the stage for meaningful business transformation. Someone needs to press PAUSE to stop the chaotic rush toward modernization and ask, "Why are we doing this?" Without doing so, businesses are only perpetuating the problem as it exists today.

In 1937, Henry Ford was quoted in Dale Carnegie's best-selling book, *How to Win Friends and Influence People*. "If there is any one secret of success, it lies in the ability to get the other person's point of view and see things from that person's angle as well as from your own."

That's what this book is about . . . getting perspective in order to find clarity and meaning in your vision.

# THE TASK FORCE, AKA STEERING COMMITTEE

It sounds like a special forces unit or a new comic book series by Marvel Comics, but instead this is your team. This is the group that you will assemble to help you begin the process of transformation to bring your vision for customer experiences and engagement to life.

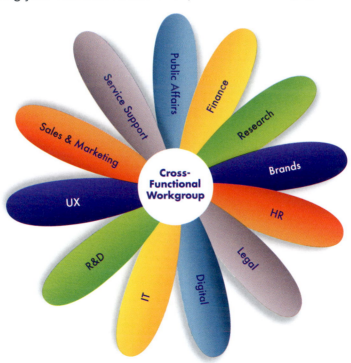

You may already have several efforts underway internally. Disruptive technology is just that—it's disruptive. Your experiential work is one of many ways your organization is getting rocked by evolution. But here, your focus is on experience, engagement, and outcomes. This will not only affect your work, but also the work of others.

For example, many organizations are investing in the development of a center of excellence for social media, digital, customer service, listening and intelligence, and collaboration. Your work spans these groups and unites them. Bringing them together around a sweeping digital or experience initiative will unite disparate teams and also disparate outcomes. Your customers don't see different departments or functions; they see one brand. The mission you're embarking on—the Hero's Journey—brings together a team that can take responsibility for not only defining, but realizing the holistic customer experience.

**Depending on the structure of your business, your task force size and shape will vary. For larger enterprises, your team may include representatives from:**

**1.** IT

**2.** Digital

**3.** UX

**4.** LoBs/brands

**5.** Legal

**6.** HR

**7.** R&D

**8.** Sales and marketing

**9.** PR/corporate communications/ public affairs

**10.** Finance

**11.** Research

**12.** Service and support

The goal of the task force is to set forth the governance and lead the charter for defining the customer experience. These distinct groups are included because in their own way each affects the customer experience. The difference is that today, the experience is disjointed as each group operates independently. For an integrated experience, think Burberry World. It takes these groups to work together to define a common vision and an accord to push forward in a common direction.

## Some of the areas of responsibility for the task force include:

- Lead dynamic customer journey (DCJ) and moment of truth (MOT) research efforts to learn
- Define the customer journey in each moment
- Design customer experiences and outcomes at every stage
- Internal stakeholder engagement to surfaces, internal opportunities, and challenges
- Champion digital strategies and the overall customer experience throughout the organization
- Develop governance model, processes, materials, and training program
- Draft experience playbook
- Draft digital engagement playbook (MOTs and DCJ)
- Provide insight on program needs based on the stakeholders they represent
- Standardize strategy development, project approvals, and success metrics
- Create checklist for businesses to review in determining prioritization for digital support
- Present progress to executive sponsors
- Prioritize, run, and measure pilots, organizations, and key stakeholders

The key here is executive sponsorship. You must enlist a connected executive, if not *the* executive, to stand behind your effort. Doing so eliminates typical barriers and also champions the movement throughout the organization. It also expedites the process and opens the door to critical, previously unattainable resources.

# THE STAGES OF CHANGE

Change is inevitable. At the same time change is daunting. Undertaking it is certainly rife with obstacles. But, merely recognizing the need to change is often the most difficult milestone to reach.

In the late 1970s, James Prochaska and Carlo DiClemente of the University of Rhode Island developed the Transtheoretical Model[1] of Behavior Change. The goal was to assess an individual's readiness to shed bad habits and to act on new, healthier behavior. The model provided strategies and processes to guide individuals through each stage to achieve and manage their goals. The stages describe a person's motivational readiness or progress toward modifying behavior.

In the Transtheoretical Model (TTM), the addressed behavior was typically problematic and the process was designed to break those bad habits. I include it here because it has its merits for organizational transformation. If nothing else, it helps provide you with the basis for a framework to chart a path forward with notable milestones and hurdles.

Prior to the TTM model, behavior change was viewed as an event, such as quitting smoking, drinking, or overeating. It's the equivalent of saying "Let's change." Prochaska's and DiClemente's model suggests that change is a process involving five distinct stages (sourced from "The Transtheoretical Model of Health Behavior Change," *Science of Health Promotion* 12, no. 1 [September/October, 1997]):[2]

**1** **Precontemplation (Not Ready):** The stage in which people are not intending to take action in the foreseeable future, usually measured as the next six months. People may be in this stage because they are uninformed or underinformed about the consequences of their behavior. Or they may have tried to change a number of times and have become demoralized about their ability to change.

**2** **Contemplation (Getting Ready):** The stage in which people are intending to change in the next six months. They are more aware of the pros of changing but are also acutely aware of the cons. This balance between the costs and benefits of changing can produce profound ambivalence that can keep people stuck in this stage for long periods of time.

**3** **Preparation (Ready):** The stage in which people are intending to take action in the immediate future, usually measured as the next month. They have typically taken some significant action in the past year. These individuals have a plan of action.

**4** **Action (Action):** The stage in which people have made specific overt modifications within the past six months. The action stage is also the stage where vigilance against relapse is critical.

**5** **Maintenance (Maintenance):** The stage in which people are working to prevent relapse but they do not apply change processes as frequently as do people in action. They are less tempted to relapse and increasingly more confident that they can continue their change.

Understanding the stages of change is helpful in constructing our plan for transformation. But a key question emerges that without an answer may stall the process before it gets any notable traction. "How do people move from one stage to another?"

In the TTM, efficacy is driven by the individual. In your work, change will have to be pushed by you and your task force. Think of yourself as the sponsor for change, someone who shepherds the process. For without you, those individuals and also the systems and processes that need to change will either relapse or abandon the effort. Self-efficacy won't apply wholeheartedly. People will need a different push in each stage to help them progress. With that said, learn from the following elements to ensure productive progress:

- Ensure the appropriate Decision Balance: A growing awareness that the advantages (the pros) of changing outweigh the disadvantages (the cons).

- Instill confidence that they can make and maintain changes in situations that tempt them to return to their old, unhealthy behavior.

- Put in place strategies that can help them make and maintain change. In the TTM model, the 10 Processes of Change include:

  1. Consciousness raising—Increasing awareness via information, case studies, proof points, and feedback.

  2. Dramatic relief—Feeling fear, anxiety, or worry because of the existing behavior, or feeling inspiration and hope when hearing about how others are able to change.

  3. Self-reevaluation—Realizing that change is an important part of who they are and want to be.

  4. Environmental reevaluation—Realizing how existing behavior affects others and how change could lead to positive effects.

  5. Self-liberation—Believing that one can change and the commitment and recommitment to act on that belief.

  6. Social liberation—Realizing that society is more supportive of change (in this case your customers and employees).

7. Helping relationships—Finding people who are supportive of change.

8. Counterconditioning—Learning about and practicing more productive behaviors to substitute the current behavior.

9. Reinforcement management—Increasing the rewards that come from positive behavior and reducing those that come from negative behavior. In the original journal, this was referred to as contingency management, which provides consequences for taking steps in a particular direction.

10. Helping relationships—Combining caring, trust, openness, and acceptance as well as support for productive behavior change.

# THE HERO'S JOURNEY

Before we take these next steps, let's revisit Chapter 2 for a moment and reacquaint ourselves with the Hero's Journey. We originally reviewed the Hero's Journey in the context of storytelling and how your customer is really at the center of the experience you're trying to create. In our closing chapter, let's use the Hero's Journey to think through the cycle of change that faces your organization. The key difference is that here, you are the hero and this is your journey. As the change agent, let's merge the TTM with the Hero's Journey to prepare you for what change will look like within your organization. Here, you are the hero.

The Hero's Journey for Transformation is divided into 4 stages and 11 phases.[3]

# STAGE 1: INCEPTION

Here you experience Total Recall. You question why? You start to see the need for change. Your initial work is focused but not yet transformational. You feel as if more can be done. But then you're not sure it's your responsibility or within your realm to push forward. Or perhaps the opportunity is bigger than you originally envisioned. You question your calling. Perhaps you even refuse it. But that's when you meet someone or others like you who will empower you . . . stand by you through the need for change. This can and should include an executive sponsor and the task force we reviewed at the end of Chapter 15.

# STAGE 2: TRIBULATION

Change is met with hardship. It's unavoidable. In this stage you start to feel the discomfort associated with leaving your comfort zone. But you're already underway. You must find a new comfort zone. As you begin the transformation process with your task force you will meet many obstacles. They'll arise in the form of resource and budget constraints, politics, skepticism, tunnel vision, and blatant ignorance. Stay true. Stay focused. Your mission serves a higher purpose and your connected customers (and employees) are anxious for you to succeed.

# **STAGE 3:** TRANSFORMATION

As the task force does its job, part of the tangential benefits include the buzz and excitement that permeates the halls of your business. Once your connected employees hear about what you're working on and what you're trying to do, they start to inquire about how they can be part of it or how soon they'll see the fruits of your efforts. This contributes to the consensus among your peers and also among decision makers.

To hold consensus takes frameworks and processes. This stage is dedicated to governance and the definition of how the organization will and will not transform. This work sets the stage for how people, teams, philosophies, and technology strategies will support the transformation.

It's always darkest before the dawn of transformation. There will be pushback. There will be more and more challenges and tasks that emerge along the way. Change is perpetual. This is where the greatest risk for a relapse exists. You must keep the team strong to prevent anyone from giving up. You've come too far for that.

# [ STAGE 4: REALIZATION ]

To call this the last stage would be a bit misleading. In the face of disruptive technology, transformation is continual. It becomes part of your business model. In this phase the team moves beyond the definition of governance to a stage of learning. In many cases I've studied, businesses develop all supporting processes and systems models around specific pilot programs. This keeps the process of change focused. More importantly, it keeps the process of change focused on learning. Here you learn and adapt accordingly. As you do, you lift your head and notice that the people inside and outside of the organization are noticing the change you've worked so diligently to realize. That, in and of itself, is rewarding to you. But, change is now constant. Take this moment to revel in your journey. Since you are the hero in this story, your journey is only beginning.

# THANK YOU

The result is a new organizational philosophy playbook to support it. This is a playbook for business transformation and the processes that support the experience—the integrated experience, relationships, and the outcomes you've designed.

And thus the Hero's Journey, your journey, begins. You and I have spent a short while together, but the lessons learned together will have a lasting impact on your career and your organization. There's much to do. From Monomyths to Total Recall to MOTs to Generation C to the dynamic customer journeys, we walk away from this experience focused on the experience. This isn't an easy task. You will face a great but rewarding road ahead. But you are not alone in this endeavor. Legions of connected customers and employees are waiting for you to make the move they've hoped for or called for. Change is in the air and thankfully it is not change for the sake of change, but instead change for the opportunity to earn and re-earn relevance and leadership. This is your calling. This is your journey. This is your time.

## #IamtheExperience

### THIS IS NOT THE END

When I get to the end of a book, I find myself gratified that I finished it. But, I also feel a pleasant sense of sorrow as I'm not always ready for the journey to end. Well, it doesn't end here. As a special thank you, I've written a bonus chapter that you can download for free right now: www .briansolis.com/WTF.

The chapter focuses on a key aspect of the formula: business + design = intended experiences. Measurement is everything. And, often how we measure results has more to do with satisfaction, sentiment, conversions and others sales, marketing, and service related numbers. What if we measured shared experiences instead of or in addition to what we do today?

Download "Measuring the Value of Shared Experiences" here: www.briansolis.com/WTF.

# [ NOTES ]

## CHAPTER 1

1. www.briansolis.com/2012/02/sorry-were-closed-the-rise-of-digital-darwinism/
2. www.endofbusiness.com/
3. www.forbes.com/sites/nathanfurr/2011/04/21/big-business-the-end-is-near/

## CHAPTER 2

1. www.amazon.com/Thousand-Faces-Collected-Joseph-Campbell/dp/1577315936/ref=sr_1_1?ie=UTF8&qid=13447 16006&sr=8–1&keywords=hero+thousand+faces

## CHAPTER 3

1. http://briansolis.posterous.com/infographic-generation-y-and-facebook
2. www.bazaarvoice.com/blog/2012/01/24/infographic-millennials-will-change-the-way-you-sell/
3. www.briansolis.com/2010/03/the-future-of-broadcast-media-is-social/
4. http://networkingexchangeblog.att.com/small-business/meet-the-new-generation-of-customersgeneration-c/
5. www.briansolis.com/2012/04/meet-generation-c-the-connected-customer/

## CHAPTER 4

1. www.washingtonpost.com/national/on-innovations/corporate-america-meet-generation-c/2012/06/27/gJQAQlKG9V_story.html
2. www.briansolis.com/2012/04/the-6-pillars-of-social-commerce-understanding-the-psychology-of-engagement/
3. http://networkingexchangeblog.att.com/small-business/the-broken-link-of-social-customer-service-part-2/
4. www.briansolis.com/2011/11/how-to-make-customer-service-matter-again-part-2/
5. www.briansolis.com/2012/04/at-your-service-versus-yourservice/

## CHAPTER 5

1. http://networkingexchangeblog.att.com/small-business/the-dim-light-at-the-end-of-the-funnel/

## CHAPTER 6

1. www.americanrhetoric.com/speeches/mlkihaveadream.htm
2. www.wirespring.com/dynamic_digital_signage_and_interactive_kiosks_journal/articles/Using_in_store_advertising_to_win_the_First_Moment_of_Truth__FMOT_-247.html
3. www.zeromomentoftruth.com

## CHAPTER 7

1. www.thinkwithgoogle.com/insights/library/studies/the-zero-moment-of-truth-macro-study

## CHAPTER 8

1. www.briansolis.com/2012/08/without-a-strategy-there-is-no-roi/
2. http://corp.crowdtap.com/#peer-influence

## CHAPTER 9

1. www.web-strategist.com/blog/2012/05/21/altimeter-research-theme-the-dynamic-customer-journey/
2. http://networkingexchangeblog.att.com/small-business/the-dim-light-at-the-end-of-the-funnel/
3. www.mckinseyquarterly.com/The_consumer_decision_journey_2373

## CHAPTER 10

1. www.briansolis.com/2011/11/how-to-make-cusotmer-service-matter-again
2. http://maritzresearch.com/~/media/Files/MaritzResearch/e24/ExecutiveSummaryTwitterPoll.ashx
3. http://thenextweb.com/socialmedia/2012/04/03/on-twitter-big-brands-like-the-gap-struggle-to-keep-up-with-customer-service/
4. www.lithium.com/pdfs/casestudies/Lithium-giffgaff-Case-Study.pdf
5. www.prnewswire.com/news-releases/multi-award-winning-giffgaff-enjoys-storming-six-months-159835575.html

## CHAPTER 11

1. http://voices.yahoo.com/that-70s-shampoothe-best-retro-shampoos-1970s-5441625.html

## CHAPTER 12

1. www.briansolis.com/2012/03/social-media-is-about-social-science-not-technology/
2. www.briansolis.com/2011/10/i-like-you-but-just-not-in-that-way/

3. www.briansolis.com/2011/04/how-do-you-increrase-social-influence-dont-think-about-the-score/
4. www.briansolis.com/2011/04/the-curation-economy-and-the-three-3c%E2%80%99s-of-information-commerce/
5. www.briansolis.com/2012/01/likes-genre-action-facebook-introduces-clicks-to-action/
6. www.amazon.com/Influence-Psychology-Persuasion-Business-Essentials/dp/006124189X/ref=la_B000AP9KKG_1_1?ie=UTF8&qid=1350873183&sr=1-1
7. www.youtube.com/watch?v=_4ZcStMsss8
8. http://trust.edelman.com/trust-download/infographic-trust-in-media/

## CHAPTER 13

1. www.washingtonpost.com/national/on-innovations/digital-darwinism-and-why-brands-die/2011/11/20/gIQAR2jqlN_story.html
2. www.briansolis.com/2012/03/the-importance-of-brand-in-an-era-of-digital-darwinism/
3. www.youtube.com/watch?v=OYecfV3ubP8
4. www.youtube.com/watch?v=PYP1Tjgt1Ao&noredirect=1
5. www.youtube.com/watch?v=vmG9jzCHtSQ&feature=player_embedded#!
6. www.theatlantic.com/business/archive/2011/05/the-worlds-most-valuable-and-fastest-growing-brands/238697/#slide10
7. www.theatlantic.com/business/archive/2011/05/the-worlds-most-valuable-and-fastest-growing-brands/238697/#slide10

## CHAPTER 14

1. www.fastcompany.com/1815756/why-user-experience-critical-customer-relationships

## CHAPTER 15

1. www.briansolis.com/2012/04/disruptive-technology-and-how-to-compete-for-the-future/
2. www.briansolis.com/2011/10/cmos-are-at-the-crossroads-of-emerging-and-disruptive-technology/
3. www.briansolis.com/2012/03/10-tenets-to-survive-digital-darwinism/
4. www.briansolis.com/2011/10/see-what-others-dont/
5. www-935.ibm.com/services/us/cmo/cmostudy2011/cmo-registration.html
6. www.briansolis.com/2011/10/is-social-media-is-an-oxymoron/
7. www.briansolis.com/2011/02/an-audience-with-an-audience-of-audiences/
8. www.briansolis.com/2010/11/it-takes-a-human-touch-no-really/
9. www.briansolis.com/2011/09/be-careful-what-you-ask-for-you-just-might-measure-it/
10. www.briansolis.com/2011/09/whats-the-r-o-i-a-framework-for-social-analytics/

11. www.briansolis.com/2012/02/facebook-files-s-1-for-5-billion-ipo-revealing-stats-revenue/
12. http://pandodaily.com/2012/01/31/delighting-the-highly-social-customer-part-1/

## CHAPTER 16

1. http://pewinternet.org/Reports/2012/Digital-differences.aspx
2. www.clickz.com/clickz/column/2184866/social-media-marketing-brand-embrace
3. www.salesforce.com/customers/stories/burberry.jsp
4. http://tech.fortune.cnn.com/2012/06/05/burberry-angela-ahrendts/

## CHAPTER 17

1. www.uri.edu/research/cprc/TTM/detailedoverview.htm
2. www.uri.edu/research/cprc/Publications/PDFs/ByTitle/The%20Transtheoretical%20model%20of%20Health%20behavior%20change.pdf
3. www.freenew.net/windows/change-management-cycle-software-20/23346.htm